For the **Love** of Cities

THE LOVE AFFAIR BETWEEN PEOPLE AND THEIR PLACES

By

PETER KAGEYAMA

Published by Creative Cities Productions

ISBN: 0615430430
ISBN-13: 9780615430430
Library of Congress Control Number: 2010942754

Acknowledgements:

Writing seems like a solitary task but this book has proven to be an effort that has been touched by many people over a long period of time. Some of them were helping me to write this long before I ever knew I was going to write a book!

Thank you to:
Michelle Royal, Charles Landry, Larry Quick, Giorgio Di Cicco, Richard Florida, Rana Florida, John Howkins, Michelle Bauer, Bob Devin Jones, Phil Cooley, Claire Nelson, Rodgers Frantz, Chris Miller, Eric Cedo, Grace Wilson, Kim Huston, Paul Schutt, Brian Boyle, Ashley Aidenbaum, Karen Gagnon, Gary Heidel, Jodi Willobee, Kate Daughdrill, Vanessa Miller, Trevor Douglas, Robert Fogarty, Shawn Micallef, Craig Christie, Tom Wujec, Rebecca Ryan, Phil Holoubek, Marnie Holoubek, Nathan Cryder, Jay McChord, Anthony "Downtown Brown" Wright, Scott Clark, Barbara Hubbard, Jeff Vines, Randy Vines, Kwende Kefentse, Russ Crumley, Hallie Bram, Sarah Szurpicki, Carol Coletta, Tim Jones, Anamaria Wills, Keith Evans & the CIDA team, Carla Fonseca, Bill Strickland, Deanne Roberts, Tom Butler, Seamus McAleavey, Mike Lydon, Cherylyn Tompkins, Kim Finn, Tom Brown, Herb Snitzer,

Diana Lind, Jennifer Thomas, Dan Gilmartin, Arnold Weinfeld, Sean Mann, Lou Musante, Tony Collins, Laura Williams, Chris Steinocher, Nancy Loehr, Debra Hensley, Kirsha Kaechele, Teresa Greenlees, Julia Gorzka, Jason Busto, Christine Harris, Tony Michaelides, Nathan Schwagler for additional research, Brad Askew for the book design, my fabulous editor Megan Voeller, Ken Walker, my sister Amy and my Mom Molly.

Special thanks to some folks who are no longer here with us but live on in the lessons they taught and the gifts they gave me: My father Paul Kageyama, my grandmother Gladys Hazen and my brother in spirit David Honeycutt. Each of them shaped me in profound ways and I carry their spirits with me every day.

The heart is a bloom.
Shoots up through the stony ground.
- U2, *Beautiful Day*

Overturning a previously accepted paradigm does not come about simply from gathering new facts that call the paradigm into question. Mere logic does not suffice to change people's minds. Against logic scientists often cling to old models until their grasps are finally loosened by something other than logic, something far deeper and more difficult to articulate that we call by various names: emotion, the irrational, the metaphysical. Or faith.
- Thomas Kuhn, *The Structure of Scientific Revolutions* – 1962

Love is the ultimate act of faith.
- Peter Kageyama - 2010

Intro

Collectively we have been having conversations about how to make cities more livable for many years now. In pursuit of livability, we routinely invoke the importance of a better built environment, more cultural amenities, increased economic opportunity, and preservation of the natural ecosystem. Livable is good—it's a fine aspiration that we have yet to achieve on any large scale. But I think we can do better.

Instead of merely livable, I think we need to start thinking about how we make our cities more lovable. I don't mean this in a "kum bay yah" kind of way, nor am I suggesting it's as simple as "let's all just get along." Rather, I'm advocating for the importance of deepening the relationships that we have with our cities and that our cities have with us. When we love something, we cherish it; we protect it; we do extraordinary things for it. When we are loved, we flourish as people and are enabled to achieve great things. This mutual love affair between people and their place is one of the most powerful influences in our lives, yet we rarely think of it in terms of a relationship. I believe that needs to change.

If cities begin thinking of themselves as engaged in a relationship with their citizens, and if we as citizens begin to consider our emotional connections with our places, we open up new possibilities in community, social and economic development by including the most powerful of motivators—the human heart—in our toolkit of city-making. This book is an effort to wrap my head around what it means to have a relationship with a place, why it matters, how such a relationship grows, how it can die, and how to better understand it. It is about understanding those rare individuals who are "in love" with a place and how they shape those places by the expression of that love.

What follows here is about renewing our love affair with our places and the incredible things that can happen when more of us fall in love with our cities. I have seen what happens when people find that emotional connection to their city and the impact on their place and on them is amazing. It is my hope that the stories and examples here inspire you to a better understanding of the relationship you have with your place. It is my hope that the official leadership of cities add "love" to their vocabulary and their repertoire of development tools and we bring the creativity, innovation and good will of our citizenry into a joint process of city building.

Chapter One
Why Lovable Cities Matter

I did not become interested in or even aware, really, of cities until my mid-thirties. I was too busy running a small web development firm with my best friend. It was the mid 90s, and everything was moving very fast in the tech sphere. We grew from our apartment to an office space in Tampa with 16 people working for us. During that time, I paid almost no attention to local politics, to local issues, to development or to anything much beyond the immediate sphere that was my business environment. My interest in community was limited to my local taxes, the quality of my school district and whether my neighbors were keeping up their lawn. I consumed my city like it was an all-you-can-eat buffet where I could pick and choose what I liked and leave the rest. In other words, I was a pretty typical community resident.

Did I love my community? When I was asked on a plane where I lived, I would say St. Petersburg or Tampa Bay, Florida. When people heard I was from Florida, they would typically say, "Oh, we love Florida." "Me, too," I would reply reflexively. I really did not think much about why I "loved" my community, and I am not sure I even really did. Like most people, I took my relationship with my community for granted, and it went unexamined.

That changed in 2003 when I first met Richard Florida, author *Rise of the Creative Class* and current head of the Martin Prosperity Institute at the University of Toronto and heard him speak about creativity and our cities. Whether you agree or disagree with him, whether you love or hate him, you cannot deny that Florida is the most recognized North American voice on this topic and has been an incredible "fire-starter" for getting people to think about cities. That may be his most enduring legacy–taking the ideas of city-building out of the hands of architects, planners and politicians, and empowering and emboldening dilettantes like me to start getting involved in their cities.

Over the next couple of years, I got to know many other thinkers and practitioners who helped shape my burgeoning thinking on cities and communities. Larry Quick from Australia and the U.K.'s Charles Landry, author of *The Creative City*, were of tremendous help. But it wasn't until late in 2005 that I finally heard something that would forever change the way I think, talk about and even experience cities.

SPEAKING POETICALLY

I was working with Charles Landry and had helped him put together a North American speaking tour that included Philadelphia, New Orleans and, as a final stop, Toronto. Charles' talk on the creative city was slated to take place in the iconic Toronto City Hall. Their main chamber seats several hundred, and the evening talk had attracted a nearly full house. Mayor David Miller opened the event and spoke powerfully and eloquently about the importance of creativity, arts and culture to the city. One would expect the mayor of a global city like to

Toronto to be able to deliver this message, and Miller certainly did not disappoint. As he concluded, he invited a tall, thin man from the dais to speak. He introduced Pier Giorgio Di Cicco, then the poet laureate of the City of Toronto. My world was about to get rocked.

Di Cicco, an Italian-born priest, had only been recently appointed to the post of poet laureate, yet he was already breaking new ground and redefining what had been a largely symbolic post. He made the role of poet laureate into an active post that was meant to reflect on and even shape the consciousness of the city. He has since become a dear friend and constant inspiration, but that night he was simply an unknown poet in a foreign city.

Di Cicco began by saying that instead of reciting a poem, he would speak poetically. Over the next 10 minutes he cast a spell with his baritone voice in that grand chamber. He talked about something so important, so basic and so primal that I was shocked to my core by the glaring absence of its mention in the past. He spoke of love. He spoke of the love we have for each other and our communities. He spoke of that love like it was an active relationship–the kind you might have with a significant other, a parent or a child. He spoke of the importance of beauty and of arts and culture to a city, and then he said something I will never forget.

"Arts and culture are what make a city fall in love with itself," he intoned. I could have wept. In that evocation, he ignited my imagination. The way I thought about cities would never be the same. Why aren't we falling in love with our cities? Why weren't more people talking about love and how to increase the love in our communities? Are we afraid of using that word in our serious discussions about city making? Why?

Since then, I have done many presentations of my own, talking about the importance of creativity and innovation to communities. In almost all of them, I quote Giorgio. And in all of them I use the word "love" because I think it's a word that needs to be used a hell of lot more when it comes to our cities.

Think about it. We don't hear "love" being mentioned in council meetings or at the planning commission or in the zoning hearings. We hear politicians use love in a simplistic, almost patriotic way when they say they "love" community. It reminds me of how easily we say that we love fried chicken or our local football team; it doesn't seem very meaningful. Yet love is one of the most basic and powerful motivations in our cosmology. It is something all of us can understand and relate to, and yet it is conspicuously absent from our conversation about community building.

But why? Is it unmanly or undignified to talk about our emotions in the public realm? Perhaps the traditionally male-dominated world of politics, architecture and planning has conspired to sterilize our conversations about cities. "We experience cities emotionally, yet we talk about them technically," says Charles Landry, author of *The Creative City*. As we have built our cities we have done so in a mechanical way, thinking about the city as a machine when it is far more of a complex living organism. Yet our solutions to building better cities often feel like we are fixing a car. I believe it's time to align our aspirations and vision with our rhetoric and accept that emotions, particularly love, can and must play a key role in the future direction of our cities.

WHY LOVABLE CITIES MATTER

We see the benefits of love in everything. When children, pets, plants and even objects are loved, they thrive. (Yes, even objects. Compare the car owned by a car lover to the cars owned by the rest of us!) The same is true of our places. When we love our city, as when we love another person, we will go to extraordinary lengths for them. We will sacrifice for them; we will push ourselves for them; we will tolerate their shortfalls; we will forgive their excesses–all because we see their true nature. When we have an emotional connection to our place, we are less likely to leave it and far more likely to champion and defend it in the face of criticism. We will fight for it. Richard Florida notes "In an economy where talent comes in all shapes, sizes and ethnicities, where the best places... have to compete for the best talent in the world, the only way to retain talent is to offer the kind of place that provides emotional attachment."[1]

His claim is supported by a survey called "Soul of the Community," recently completed by the Gallup Organization in conjunction with the John S. and James L. Knight Foundation, that investigated levels of community attachment. The survey uncovered a significant relationship between local economic growth and feelings of passion and loyalty among community residents. From 2002 to 2006, the survey found, the most "attached" communities had the highest local GDP growth. [2]

But how many of us are "in love" with our cities? Very few, apparently. Turns out it's rare to find that special love that makes people willing to do something for their places. In the "Soul of the Community" survey, only 24% of those interviewed said they were even "attached" to their community–and attached is a far cry from being in love! In the same survey, 36% of people were "neutral," and 40% said they were "unattached" to their community. That means seven in ten people essentially don't care about their community. How can this have happened? How has the relationship gotten this bad? And what can we do to fix it?

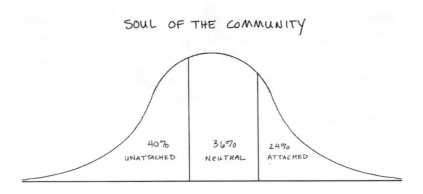

SOUL OF THE COMMUNITY

40%
UNATTACHED

36%
NEUTRAL

24%
ATTACHED

In trying to repair a relationship—any relationship—we need to understand its history and how we arrived at the current state of affairs. We need to understand what each party needs. We need to start changing behaviors and to recognize that such change is a process; we won't go from apathy or disdain to love overnight. We begin with small steps that move people towards having an emotional connection with their place.

When cities make themselves easier to connect with emotionally—when they make themselves more lovable—they invite the human heart to become a driver of community, economic and social development.

We need examples of positive relationships to help us better model our own. We need to be reminded of what it means to have a relationship with a place. To help us fall in love with our cities again, we need to see others who are in love with their communities. These people are a rare breed and, I believe, critical to the overall health of their places.

MAKING THE COMMUNITY

We tend to think of "the city" or "the community" as an entity, a single identifiable construct to which we assign attributes and characteristics much like we would a corporation or an individual. In the same way, when we look at a beach, we see it as a whole rather than as millions of grains of sand. In asking ourselves how to change a community, we need to remember that any community is made up of millions of acts, positive and negative, which at a distance become the whole we perceive. Each of us contributes to that whole. Each of us makes or breaks the city in small ways every day as we lead our lives. When we throw our soda can or cigarette butt onto the street, we diminish our community. When we hold the door for a stranger or let another car merge into our lane, we add something to the community. Small things, like the grains of sand on a beach, make up the totality of a place.

But for the most part, we consume the city. We take from its resources: parks, security, airports, roads and bike paths. Most of us consume the city without giving back, other than by being a good citizen who obeys laws, pays her taxes and, as a byproduct of consumption, spends money back into the community.

Have you ever thought about who really makes a community? About who makes the city a place that you actually want to live? Of course, the official actors (mayors, planners, nonprofit leaders, educators, community leaders and others) come to mind when we think about who makes cities. Add to that list those who perform the necessary functions of keeping the city safe and smoothly functioning. But that still does not account for what ultimately makes a community.

I believe that if you examined who really builds, contributes to and essentially "makes" a city, you would find that those citizens who have an emotional connection with their city make the difference.

The city, as a whole, is made by a relatively small number of "co-creators" who—in their roles as entrepreneurs, activists, artists, performers, students, organizers and otherwise "concerned citizens"–create the experiences that most of us consume. Many of these co-creators act without authority or centralized direction, and it is from their creative efforts that the rest of us benefit. They make the experiences that we delight in, and they have a disproportionate impact in the making of the city.

I call this small group of makers "co-creators" because they build on existing elements, like infrastructure and institutions, and collaborate with others to make new things. They are also connectors and catalysts who in turn inspire others to get involved and contribute to the making of their community.

These are people who are passionate and committed to their friends, their neighbors and their community and are the creators of the elements that make a place truly livable. This emotional connection is the difference between merely consuming the city and creating something for the city. These efforts are often small and discounted elements such as a neighborhood watch, a youth group, an effort to clean up a park or to start a new community theater. And at the extreme end of the spectrum are those people who are "in love" with their community–who do extraordinary things, sometimes intentionally, sometimes merely as a side effect of their personal passion and creativity. They fill the ever increasing gap between official action and official resources with their efforts and their presence can be the difference between a city that is "loved" and city that is merely lived in.

THE ONE PERCENT

How can a relatively small group of people create something as large as a city or a community? In the online world, Wikipedia and other virtual communities have demonstrated that a tiny proportion of members of such communities account for the vast majority of activity in the group. Social science refers to this phenomenon as "participation inequality," and statisticians call it a "power law distribution". In the online world, it has become recognized as the "one percent rule," of which Wikipedia, the online, collaboratively authored encyclopedia is a perfect example.

As of June 2010, the "open source" Wikipedia is one of the 10 most trafficked websites in the world, with over 15 million total articles (3.3 million in English) and more than 20 million pages in 270 languages. If you use the web at all, chances are you have used Wikipedia. It has become the go-to source for a digital generation that doesn't really care about the official pedigree of information or authors (i.e., volunteer contributors)–and in all likelihood, Wikipedia will someday be recognized as an authoritative source of information. It has been touted as a model of 21st century collaboration and open source development.

According to Wikipedia, its membership consists of 12,386,000 registered users and 91,000 active contributors. The ratio of active contributors, those who literally make Wikipedia, is .0073–or about three quarters of one percent. In Wikipedia's case, less than one percent of the community truly makes the community. And we consume it. Without the efforts of those active contributors, we would still be loading CD-ROMs of Microsoft's Encarta into our laptops. Even more extraordinarily, almost none of the contributors were paid for their efforts.

I asked Wikipedia founder Jimmy Wales if he was surprised that such a small group played such a big role in making Wikipedia. "Not at all," he replied. "Most of us, in most contexts are just customers of something–consumers."

The co-creators of Wikipedia believe in the central mission of Wikipedia: to create a global encyclopedia for all. They are engaged and stimulated by the experience of working on the project. And it's fun! "I think if it weren't for that enjoyment aspect, people wouldn't really do it," says Wales. Wikipedia's co-creators are more than "engaged" in the community—they have a deep connection with it. Their motivation stems from a multiplicity of unquantifiable incentives and rewards: from the project's inspiring mission to its visible results, from the relationships they build through collaboration to the sense of accomplishment they feel in building and creating something. Perhaps the best way to summarize these complex motivations and desires is to say that these people "love" Wikipedia—and I mean really love it. Wikipedia has become the locus of their creative energies, their desire to build and their need to make a difference.

The same type of fans, supporters and co-creators exist in every city, and in my travels over the past few years I have been lucky enough to meet many of them. They are an extraordinary lot—wildly diverse but sharing the common threads of a strong emotional connection with, sometimes even true love for, their place and the desire to make things happen.

I have seen such people do amazing things that have profound impact on their communities, and I have seen how they are largely misunderstood and misused by communities. I have come to think of them as a new and fabulous natural resource that we just haven't figured out yet how to channel into our conventional engines.

This small group of people in love with their cities—they are the "unobtanium" of communities (to borrow a concept from the blockbuster movie *Avatar*). They are more precious than gold and just as rare. They represent an incredibly powerful force for change in communities and, in turn, communities depend upon them, though perhaps unknowingly. In fact, small increases or small losses of these people may ultimately be the difference between cities that thrive and cities that wilt and die. Communities need to ask themselves who these champions in their midst are, how to increase their numbers and most important, how do we keep them engaged in our city.

Chapter Two
The Affair and Why It Ended

How did we arrive at a situation where more than 75% of us do not feel any connection with our places? James Kunstler, author of *The Geography of Nowhere: The Rise and Decline of America's Man-Made Landscape*, has said we have "created places not worth caring about,"[3] but that did not happen overnight. To better understand our relationship with our places we need to look at where we came from.

In the United States, in the late 19th and early 20th century we romanticized the idea of the city. The idea of the city captured our imaginations. They were what was next and what held the promise of the future. Think about that time- cities were electrifying themselves and bringing light and power everywhere. Telephones brought communications to the masses. The industrial revolution was creating jobs, money, power and a new urban way of life. At its heart there was opportunity. Opportunity to make things and to not be a servant to the land.

The honeymoon period of course did not last. The "affair" had grown stale and, while we did not hate our cities in the 30's, 40's, and 50's, we did neglect them. And like unloved toys they became tattered afterthoughts and items of disrepair.

WHY THE AFFAIR ENDED

After World War II we began to drift away from the notion of the city and more towards the suburbs. Years of the Great Depression followed by years of war had made us hungry for something new. Our personal manifest destiny became owning a small piece of the American dream complete with picket fences, a car, two kids and a dog. This ideal precipitated the end of the affair with our cities. And two key pieces of public policy following WWII led to these outcomes: The 1949 Federal Housing Act and the 1956 Federal Highway Act.

The 1949 Federal Housing Act began the urban renewal programs that actually decimated most urban centers. The original intention was that older housing would be destroyed and newer, low income housing would be built in its place. In practice these programs were a failure. Urban renewal became known as "negro removal"[4] and many thought "the real aim of urban renewal… was to get rid of black ghettos, the existence of which offended white people and also occupied land that was potentially valuable."[5]

Many developers used this legislation to simply remove low income residents and build higher priced, market rate properties in their stead and where low income housing was built, it was poorly designed high rises and campuses that created dense pockets of poverty. Cabrini Green in Chicago, Pruitt-Igoe in St. Louis and River Park in New York City became emblematic of these developments. From these new ghettos, crime and other social ills found fertile ground to grow.

The 1956 Federal Highway Act poured billions of federal dollars into infrastructure and increased the suburbanization of America by bringing roads to these new communities and privileging the car even further. Men like Robert Moses, the head of several public authorities in New York and the master builder of the era, wielded this act like a broadsword and used it to cleave our cities in two, destroying traditional neighborhoods and placing the car at the center of our thinking about cities. The Cross Bronx Expressway had such a devastating effect on the mostly black neighborhoods of that area that a corresponding backlash against such plans, the so-called "freeway revolts" eventually prevented Moses from putting in freeways that would have crossed Midtown and Lower Manhattan.

Additionally, federally backed mortgages were limited to new, single family dwellings, which effectively precluded all urban living.

The suburbs boomed while cities found themselves at a key "tipping point" in their existence. They were losing population as the educated, mostly white citizens fled to the suburbs, taking with them political clout and money, leaving behind urban centers that were increasingly poor and black. William Whyte, best known for his book *The Organization Man* but also one of the great urban thinkers of the 20th century wrote this in 1958:

"Will the city reassert itself as a good place to live? It will not unless there is a decided shift in the thinking of those who would remake it. The popular image of the city as it is now is bad enough – a place of decay, crime, of fouled streets, and of a people who are poor or foreign or odd."[6]

The city, he goes on to write, is "not designed by people who like cities"[7], which explains how our cities become objects of both fear and derision.

When I was kid, one of my favorite books was *From the Mixed-Up Files of Mrs. Basil E. Frankweiler* by E.L. Konigsburg. Published in 1967 it is the tale of young Claudia and her even younger brother who run away from home in the "commuting suburb" of Greenwich, Connecticut for the excitement of New

York City, specifically the Metropolitan Museum of Art. In the beginning of the book, Claudia notes that her mother and her friends in the Mah-Jong club did not like "the city" and "most of them never ventured there; it was exhausting and it made them nervous." For Claudia, the city was just the opposite: "Claudia loved the city because it was elegant; it was important; and busy."[8]

Though it was a children's book, it was an accurate portrait of the feelings many had about their major metropolitan areas. When Claudia says that the city made her mother "nervous" she was politely stating that many people, particularly the psychic middle of America, had become fearful of cities because "urban" had become synonymous with "Black." In 1967 when Konigsburg published the book, racial tension had flared up in cities from Los Angeles to Detroit to New York, with some of the worst yet to come.

The role of race and racism cannot be underestimated in the decline of our cities. Thomas Sugrue, in his brilliant history of modern Detroit, *The Origins of the Urban Crisis* focuses on Detroit, but his points about a long series of events and decisions could be applied to most post-war urban centers. Whites with the means moved en masse to the suburbs, the hollowing out process that left cities racially and economically divided even today. For Sugrue, the crisis reaches a boiling point due to many factors, ranging from unions and access to quality employment, red lining neighborhoods by banks, white flight and fear of integrated neighborhoods and schools, real estate practices that played on those fears and the emerging civil rights movement. Sugrue points out that these multiple factors, no single one of them dispositive, in combination lead up to the "crisis" that ultimately ends our love affair with urban areas all over the country.

In the decades that followed, urban disenfranchisement was made easier because the white majority felt that "urban" spending was for the primary benefit of blacks. As the white majority fled to the suburbs they took their money and notions of civic space with them. The suburbs proliferate in this era and our cities fall further into neglect and despair. (While I am focused on American cities, the pattern in post-war European cities is similar. Chasing opportunities, ethnic and racial minorities flocked to Europe's major cities, literally changing the complexion of those places. Native flight to suburban enclaves followed with the familiar hollowing out effect. In some ways, Europe is dealing with this later than the US. Look at the riots that burned Paris in the fall of 2005 to see similar themes of class, race, economic exclusion and lack of meaningful integration.)

By the 70's and 80's, the affair was officially over. Our neglect of the public realm became indicative of those feelings. *Geography of Nowhere* author James Kunstler points out that the "public realm is the physical manifestation of the common good."[9] Disinterest and disinvestment leads to a psychic disconnection for many with the urban cores of their regions. The urban/suburban rift blooms and we are left with a bitterly divided national consciousness about cities and even the word "urban."

PLACES NOT WORTH CARING ABOUT

As money, education, political influence and emotional connections moved away from urban centers into the suburbs, we created a culture of cars and sprawl with the attendant problems. The idea of the public realm devolved into the roads that connected us to shopping and our McMansions. We lost a strong sense of civic identity as our suburbs became generic at best, shockingly dull and ugly at their worst. We created vast "places not worth caring about."[10]

Kunstler goes on to say "The immersive ugliness of the everyday environment of America is entropy made visible. We can't overestimate the amount of despair we are generating."[11] In dense, walkable urban areas, the public realm was more important if for no other reason than the citizens were more connected to it. Public space means very little when you are in your car at 45mph. It means far more when you are walking through it. The unfortunate byproduct of our suburban, car-centered life has been the devolvement and loss of any sort of expectation about our cities beyond mere functionality and safety. When success is measured in getting cars from point A to point B as quickly as possible and traffic engineers have more say in how our cities look and feel, we know we have lost our way.

Kunstler raises a key point in our thinking about cities. As we have detached from the public realm, so too have we detached from out emotional connection to our city. Ugly, utilitarian spaces beget no love. Sprawling developments that require cars to maneuver reduce our connections to each other and we make it so much harder to care about anything beyond our front door. Our car has become a prophylactic that prevents us from connecting to our places.

Whether by plan or merely a byproduct, the consequence of our public policy, urban planning and design decisions was to keep people separate, isolated and in identity groups. It was a kind of architecture (and planning) against relationships.

We have created an urban hierarchy that does not aspire to anything more than utility and to be in service to the car. In this hierarchy, things such as beauty and sociality have no place. This thinking has reasserted itself with particular virulence in the economic crisis of the past few years. As budgets get slashed and tax bases shrink, the common reaction is to focus on basics at the expense of that which ultimately makes places interesting, memorable and lovable.

Now we want to get back into a more relational mode in our cities, in part because we have some distance between the overt race-centered politics of the 1960s and an increasing sense that differences and diversity are a strength. We have discovered that we have many more things in common rather than a set of "irreconcilable differences".

How do we start to care again? Many, including Kunstler would point to a reinvestment in our public spaces and I agree that that is a area ripe for re-examination and reinvestment. But with so many of our public coffers empty, it is a hard sell to get communities to spend on public works projects such as these. In this resource strapped environment we need to consider other elements that make for a strong, healthy relationship. Just as money alone does not make for great relationships, we need to consider some other, non-financial elements. Elements that often don't find their way into discourse about city building such as fun, playfulness, sentimentality, improvisation, curiosity and discovery.

CITY PYRAMID

Most people have heard the expression "Good enough for government work." It is one of those cynical expressions that we all can relate to because we tend to think of government work as banal, uninspired and workman-like at best. We have equated government work with the least common denominator and the lowest acceptable standard of performance. How sad for us that we as citizens have let our governments reach this sorry state and how tragic that governments think of themselves in these diminished terms. The result? We get cities that meet the minimum expectations and communities that do not engage us emotionally and are not worth caring much about.

In the city making "hierarchy of needs" we see most communities focused on bottom-line, core issues of making cities functional and safe. There still are many communities that struggle to even deliver functional and safe but that is not the problem. The problem is when communities only focus on the functional and safe and never raise their aspirations beyond the "good enough for government work" level. Part of this is clearly economic. As city budgets get cut, it becomes a challenge to maintain the core functions let alone aspire to higher things. But a huge part of it is mindset.

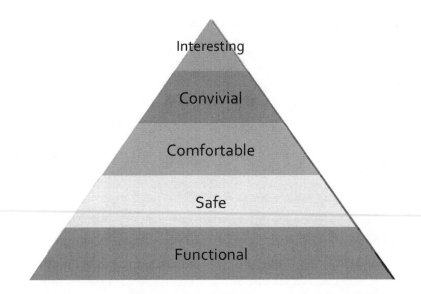

Jacques Wallage is the mayor of Groningen, a city of 188,000 in the Netherlands. He asked the people of his city what they wanted from their city and he indicated surprise at one of the primary elements. "They want more places to sit down when they are tired" which has led the city increasingly to ask "What can (the city) do to make everyone feel at ease in their city?"[12]

Why can't the city be comfortable as well as functional? Why can't the city use space and resources to build social capital among citizens and create a more convivial atmosphere? Why doesn't the city strive to be interesting and yes, even fun! If we were to buy a car we would not settle for a functional, safe box with wheels (there is an old Volvo joke in here). We think of our relationship with our car as more immediate, but the reality is that our relationship with our city is far more expansive, though largely unexamined.

If the city and the citizens see themselves in a relationship then these higher aspirations become a critical part of the equation. These are the elements that make places worth caring about, essentially making places lovable. City leaders and we as citizens have become so desensitized to place that we don't ask and don't think about making our communities comfortable, convivial and fun. My challenge to citizens and community leaders everywhere during the next city council debate or public hearing on some project, is to ask how it can be made more interesting and fun. See how that changes the conversation and the thinking!

Of course our communities must be functional and safe; that is the minimum threshold for success and for having any kind of relationship with your city. But we don't love places because they are merely functional and safe. When we start including the higher aspirations of community into the mix; comfort, conviviality, beauty and fun, we begin to make places that are beyond merely livable and may ultimately be lovable.

Chapter Three
What Is Love Anyway?

So what is love? From Plato's Symposium, to Shakespeare's sonnets, to Bridget Jones's Diary, the most creative, thoughtful and astute minds have pondered the meaning and the definitions of love. Far be it from me to recite or hope to improve upon thousands of years of writings and musings on the nature of love. What I will point out is that all of us have at least anecdotal experience with love. At some point in our lives we have loved, been loved, experienced some emotional connection to a person, place, pet or object that we would call "love." This means we all have our personal "definition" of love. My experience with love may differ from yours, but I suspect that since we are both human beings we share far more in common than not when it comes to love.

If this were an academic treatise, I would spend a lot of time and effort to define love in quantifiable terms, would then go out and measure that love in each community and build a schema that shows most-to-least-loved communities around the country. (Then I could set up a consulting practice to make cities into love black belts and charge lots of money for that!)

But I don't want to define love for you. Defining is limiting, and I cannot tell you how to love your city. I want each person, each community, to discover their own version and flavor of love. Because each version is as valid as the next and there is no technically satisfactory definition of love. Just as each human being sees color differently (we may all agree that the sky is "blue," but your blue and my blue may not be the same thing), we each experience love differently. What we probably do agree upon is the importance, the power and the general feeling that is "love." When you say you love your dog, I can relate even if I don't have a dog. When you say you love Cleveland, Ohio, I can understand—even if I have never been to Cleveland. Point of fact, I do have a dog that I love very much (Buffy if you are reading this - GOOD dog!) and as a native Ohioan, I do have love for the North Coast!

Because love is so diverse, and manifests in so many different forms, it is a strength that communities need to access. If we all had the same taste and loved the same things, our communities would become monotonous and bland. Even that which we love would become boring. It is the new, the different and the unexpected peppered in with the familiar that makes for the most interesting experiences.

HOW WE EXPERIENCE CITIES

How many times have we heard someone say how much they love a particular place? You have probably said it yourself as it is a very common discussion we have. We talk about loving a particular place (when we describe our home to others or when we return from vacation); we loved the food, the architecture, the history, the shopping, the waterfront, how we could walk everywhere, the music we heard, the colors we saw and the cool people we met. All of these experiences are essentially emotional experiences. Charles Landry, founder of the Creative City movement, has often noted that "If you talk to people about cities, it's all very emotional—it's about feelings, desire... how can you fall in love with a city."[13]   While we experience the city emotionally, our dialog about cities defaults back to highly technical, mechanical language.

In this context, language is particularly important. It sets the frame for how we think about and discuss our cities. Go to a council meeting, a planning workshop or a zoning hearing, and you will hear vast amounts of technical discussion but little about the emotional experience of a city. Notes Landry "If you think of the city as a mechanical thing... you tend to come up with mechanical solutions. If you think of the city as an organism... suddenly it's all about relationships. How do people connect? How do they work together?"[14]   But in contexts like council meetings, we act as if those terms are inappropriate to the serious work of city making.

For example, instead of testifying about floor area ratios and density bonuses, what if such conversations included what it feels like to live in denser urban areas? We should talk about greater interactions and potential connections we have with each other when we live closer proximity. We say "hi" to each other, we help each other, we build connections and we are safer because we are in a community. We are more conscientious and don't litter as much. We take care of our property more and we are happier in our community. All these things happen when we live in better-designed, denser areas. But instead the conversation is about ratios, cars and parking per resident. When we limit our conversation to the technical language, which most of us do not possess, we can miss out on what people are really feeling and what they really desire from their community.

Jay McChord is a city councilman in Lexington, Kentucky and a passionate, emotional guy. (In college he was the mascot for the University of Kentucky - the guy in the Wildcat suit!). When I asked him about this disconnect between planning and feeling, he noted that running the city has become incredibly technical because of the complexity of the operation and the requirements placed on local government by state and federal governments when funds are allocated. The reality is, people like Jay need to navigate a very technical system in order to create change. But he is careful not to squelch citizens' enthusiasm and their passion. "There was a time when all I had going for me was my enthusiasm so I recognize how important that is," he says. He strives for a balance between the necessary technicalities and the genuine heart of the matter. As a naturally passionate guy, Jay strikes the balance with relative ease. But for most communities, achieving balance would mean embracing more emotion and a more human-centered approach to the conversation around city making. I understand that this seems risky to many cities and their bureaucracies. It opens the door to the non-professional crowd but I believe the benefits they bring – excitement, enthusiasm, a willingness to work and a capacity to create change, outweighs their lack of traditional expertise. As resources become scarce, these citizens will be needed to fill the gaps that diminished funds and power have created. If we make "expertise" a hurdle to clear, we may be eliminating many, excited, well meaning but ignorant resources.

LOVE IN COMMUNITY DIALOG

Why is love out of place in community dialog? For something so central and common to our humanity, it is odd that love, beauty and happiness are not part of our everyday community conversation.

As Americans, could it be that our Puritan heritage makes us uncomfortable with public displays of emotion? Strange then since we Americans certainly appreciate having our heartstrings played. One need only look at a syrupy Olympics background story or the latest episode of Extreme Makeover Home Edition to see how we enjoy having our emotions manipulated. But you rarely see our political leaders show emotions other than token anger and outrage or the occasion display of grief when the timing is appropriate. Remember what a big deal it was when Hilary Clinton shed a tear during the Democratic Primary in 2008? That was front page news! So I ask you: Where is the love?

I am not sure of the historical antecedents of this bias but in current times there seems to be an overriding fear amongst political leaders of being seen as frivolous. As budgets tighten and hard choices must be made, programs that seem "frivolous," soft or artistic are the first cut. No one wants to vote for arts programs when we have streets that need fixing, sewers that need cleaning and parking decks that need to be built. This is an easy and convenient choice for the politicos to make as they know that most citizens (particularly the consumers of the city) are not going to question these choices.

Justifying the value of arts and culture is far more difficult, and most leaders simply don't want the bother of such contentious conversations. I suspect that this has always been the case, but certainly the economic crisis of 2008-2009 and its ongoing fallout has exacerbated this tendency. Today, economic rationalism (policy driven primarily by sound economic terms) is the norm, and we manage our cities and our companies by the bottom line. It becomes easy to say "no" to many things in this worldview, because everything is reduced down to costs with little or no consideration of the intangible value of things.

We have lumped art, culture, beauty and love into that "soft" bucket that contains terms such as liberal, compassion, social justice, equality and welfare. We have made those values into signs of weakness that even the most progressive candidates have run away from. We even saw the attempt to make "community worker" into a negative term in the last presidential election.

We need to take back "love," make it the strength that it clearly is and reframe the conversation.

DOES HAPPINESS EQUAL LOVE?

In the United Kingdom, Conservative leader David Cameron was quoted in 2006 saying that "there's more to life than money, and it's time we focused not just on GDP but on GWB - General Wellbeing."[15] Not exactly a full-throated declaration of love, but it does perhaps represent an attitudinal shift regarding our overall wellbeing. In the fall of 2010, after coming to power earlier in the year, Cameron announced a plan to start measuring happiness as a key metric of national wellbeing.[16] Despite tough economic times, the move was applauded by the other parties' leadership as well.

Still, we are beginning to embrace the idea of happiness as a worthwhile goal for communities. In the book, *The Politics of Happiness,* author Derek Bok notes that the general level of happiness in the US and other developed nations has not risen in the past 50 years despite "substantial" growth in income. We have met the basic threshold requirements for communities (functional and safe) but we have not yet figured out how to enhance the upper parts (comfort, conviviality and fun). Or to use Maslow's hierarchy, though we have achieved basic material needs, we haven't yet attained meaning and transformation.

Part of the problem, argues Bok, is that we are bad judges of what makes us happy. In particular we are "unable to predict the duration of the happiness or unhappiness brought on by many common events or changes in our lives."[17] We think that the new house or new car will make us happy but that does not last. We think that an extra 10 minutes to our commute will not make us unhappy. And we are wrong. According to Robert Putnam, author of *Bowling Alone*, that extra 10 minutes added to the average commute actually diminishes your overall quality of life by an astonishing 10%.[18]

Poets will say that love is a bittersweet pill that can make us very unhappy. Certainly popular music would suffer if love were always a happy occurrence. But broadly speaking, people doing what they love, what they are passionate about and what engages them leads to happiness. Government is not responsible for legislating happiness, but smart communities make it a little more likely to happen by their policy decisions. Communities have embraced the notion of becoming more creative and innovative because they see the economic benefits of those characteristics. So, too, should enlightened cities recognize that happiness has economic benefits; happier citizens are healthier both physically and mentally, live longer, and enjoy more success at work.[19]

PURSUING HAPPINESS

Freud believed that the pursuit of happiness was a doomed quest. Happiness is "not included in the plan of creation" he noted. Instead he aspired that we should all achieve a state of "ordinary misery." Cheerful guy. Mommy issues.

At the other end of the spectrum, the US Declaration of Independence enumerates one of the key elements of Natural

Law, that being "the pursuit of happiness," in its preamble. As a nation, we are founded on this principle.

For purposes of community/city building, happiness is a key aspirational goal. Social capital coming from social interactions and the resulting connections are the key to happiness. This can be as simple as increasing our time being around other people. Researchers "have concluded that human relationships and connections of all kinds contribute more to happiness than anything else."[20]

Cities that find ways to increase the opportunities and the potential quality of interactions among its citizens will create happier people and, thus, happier places. If a city settles for merely making sure that it provides a functional and safe environment, it misses the opportunity to create happier citizens by making a more convivial environment. And if it fails to make its citizens happier, they will likely be less healthy and less productive in their work, and the community as a whole will suffer for it. I am not suggesting that cities put their citizens on the psychiatric couch or start putting Prozac in the water. I am urging that cities start thinking about, and planning for, the emotional dimension of the city-citizen relationship.

Chapter Four
The Continuum of
Engagement

The Soul of the Community is a three-year study, funded by the John S. and James L. Knight Foundation and conducted by the Gallup organization, which explores the community qualities that influence residents' loyalty and passion for where they live and how those feelings relate to indicators of community well-being such as local economic growth. During the course of the study, over 28,000 people in 26 cities were interviewed, and three key aspects of community consistently turned up as the "magic ingredients"[21] to community satisfaction.

The three keys:

#3 – AESTHETICS

As part of their process, "Gallup researchers asked residents two questions about its attractiveness - how they rated the area's parks, playgrounds and trails and how they rated its overall beauty and physical setting. It turns out a pretty city is a lovable city."[22]

The researchers noted that great design features such as New York City's High Line Park (see "Love Notes" in Chapter Seven) added tremendously to the overall satisfaction that residents had with their community. I am a big fan of High Line Park and I would argue that such design features have a disproportionate impact on the love and affection we have for our places. In the grand scheme of NYC, High Line Park is a small element and one that most New Yorkers will not use on a daily or weekly basis. But knowing it is there is still immensely satisfying to the community and clearly a reason to love the city.

In the 2009 update to the survey, the highest rated city was Bradenton/Sarasota in Florida. Residents listed the aesthetics of their community, particularly their parks and natural spaces as most significant. By contrast, the residents of the lowest ranked city– Gary, Indiana– listed their highways as their most significant aesthetic asset.

But lack of great aesthetics does not preclude your being a lovable city. One need only visit Austin, TX to see that it is aesthetically dull, even ugly, in many places. Yet Austin continually ranks amongst the most creative, admired and livable cities. Lack of aesthetics is not disqualifying; it merely means you have to work harder in other areas.

#2 SOCIAL OFFERINGS

For their second major finding, Gallup researchers asked residents about "how fun and social their communities are - Is there vibrant nightlife? Is it a good place to meet people and make friends? How much do residents seem to care about each other?"[23]

Fun is not something most cities plan. Yet, clearly, it is incredibly important in our measurement of lovable communities. Cities need to encourage social offerings and activities and lessen procedural impediments so that citizens use the city as a venue more than they themselves need to create the offerings. Certainly some things should be produced and executed by the city (Fourth of July Fireworks for example), but mostly these experiences should be done by non-city agents. I don't really want to see the city's production of Macbeth or Rent but I appreciate that the local theater companies use the city parks for their summer productions of these shows.

#1 OPENNESS

The number one trait and the one "identified as decisive in determining residents' attachment to a community was openness. To get at this trait, researchers asked whether the community was a "good place for" different groups of people - senior citizens, racial and ethnic minorities, families with kids, gays and lesbians, college graduates, and immigrants from other countries."[24]

Richard Florida likewise determined that "Tolerance" (his measure of openness) was key to the long-term economic success of communities.[25] But what is about openness and tolerance that we really value?

At the most basic level, openness reflects the notion that if people are cool with those other folks looking or acting differently, they will be OK with me and my differences. For that group of co-creators we talked about, openness is synonymous with opportunity; the opportunity to make a difference, make changes, to create something different, unusual or untried and push it into the consciousness of the community. That is far more challenging than being tolerant and diverse. It is easy to say we are open to new people until they start changing things!

CAN YOU RUN FOR MAYOR?

When trying to measure the openness of a community, I often like to ask whether or not this is the type of community that I could move to, get engaged and in five or ten years run for mayor. This seems to be a pretty good barometer. Cities that are too small and too insular, where you have to be born there and even after 20 years you are still a newcomer, are not going to let an "outsider" become mayor. Likewise cities that are too big don't allow you to climb the corridors of power that quickly. Try to go to NYC or Chicago and run for mayor. Unless you are a billionaire, you will most likely find that option closed to you.

Big cities are tolerant but not necessarily as open as others because of those entrenched power systems. And the expense of bigger cities makes them problematic for many. This is why I believe we need to expand our thinking on the term "openness" beyond the tolerance and diversity aspect. Places need to be open to your creative and entrepreneurial energies. They need to open to your imprint and efforts and welcome your contributions. Openness needs to include the possibility of you making a contribution to the place. If housing is hugely expensive, or there are highly established corridors of power or if class hierarchies feel fixed and immutable, it is much harder to feel like there is room for you to contribute to the community.

For many, big cities are wonderful because they are tolerant and allow (and encourage) infinite varieties of consumption. Come and be part of the party they say; enjoy yourself and have a drink. But for those wishing to throw their own party, these places may prove to be more problematic—not because of any overt hostility or intolerance but simply due to costs, tradition and scale.

THE CONTINUUM OF ENGAGEMENT

The Soul of the Community survey found that 40% of us are "not engaged" with our communities, with 36% of us "neutral" and only 24% of us "engaged" with our places. But what does that really mean, and how can communities use this information to try to better engage their citizens? Part of the challenge I see is that this data lumps community champions who are passionately engaged with their cities into the attached group , which also includes well meaning citizens who attend the occasional community meeting and volunteer at their church.   The degree and the intensity to which people are involved matters here.   So too at the other end, where we see people who are not engaged with their community.   Are they actively looking to relocate or are they, like most, just bored? While I find this survey incredibly informative, its categories strike me as big nets that scoop up different kinds of people; when we say someone is "engaged," in the terms of this poll, we're really talking about people with very different levels of engagement. If we're going to take these numbers and translate them into city-changing actions, we need to appreciate those subtle gradations of difference (more subtle than the terms of the survey). That's why I created a continuum, or a curve, based on those numbers.

The "Continuum of Engagement" is more representative of our levels of commitment and passion for our places, but is actually representative of our relationship with just about anything or anyone.   This could be applied to your city, your spouse, Starbucks or your local sports franchise.

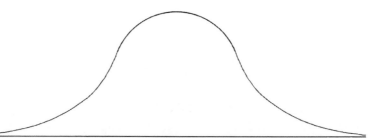

CONTINUUM OF ENGAGEMENT

HOSTILE   ANGRY   DETACHED   BORED   NEUTRAL   CURIOUS   ENGAGED   COMMITTED   LOVE

The key point here is that this diagram should look like a pretty standard bell curve– with most of us in the middle and decreasing numbers of people falling to the extremes on either side. If we were able to take the Soul of the Community survey and ask the respondents where they fell on the curve, I think we would find some interesting distinctions.

For example, 40% of those surveyed said they were not attached to their community. I submit that the majority of that group falls closer to the center and are not actually hostile or angry towards the community, but rather just bored. They are not stimulated by their environment, their peers or their work– and the city gets the blame for that. Fewer are detached and fewer still angry at their city. Perhaps the community has done something that is personally disappointing and they hold that against the city. At the tail end of the continuum are those very few who are actively hostile to the place and seeking to get out. Similarly, those who are attached to the community are most likely curious and interested in what is going on around them. They are not passionate champions who are going to create a new street festival or start a Facebook group that celebrates cycling in the city. They are simply engaged citizens who find things that interest them in their networks. Again, the city can take some of the credit for that.

At the far end of the positive side of the continuum you will find those co-creators of the place. They are passionate and committed to their city –some would even say they are in love with their place. They are the "secret sauce" or the "magic dust" that makes a significant difference in their communities. This very small group is responsible for an outsized portion of the content that the rest of us consume. They make things, and they make things happen.

In St. Petersburg, we have a fantastic community arts project called the Studio@620. Founded in 2004, the Studio has grown from very humble beginnings to being one of the most influential arts groups in the region, due in large part to its creative director, Bob Devin Jones. Bob is a transplant from Los Angeles and a self-described lover of St. Pete. His voicemail message used to end with "This is St. Petersburg!" Beyond the Studio, Bob is literally everywhere: on different boards of directors, in meetings, occasionally performing and directing. He is a central node in the network that makes St. Petersburg. But he would not show up on any official organizational chart of city staffers or affiliates. Bob is a co-creator of the community and an incredible resource, and if you look in your own city, you will find a few others like him as well.

Bob Devin Jones, Creative Director, Studio@620, St. Petersburg, FL

When a community gains one of these co-creators, they gain far more than one person. They gain a maker, an influencer, a catalyst and an anchor persona for the community. When a community loses a co-creator, they lose all that and perhaps even more; they lose all the future things that person will make for another community. Economic development offices track the comings and goings of businesses and jobs, but who is tracking this small group of makers and ensuring that they do not leave or become disenchanted with their city? If a major employer were about to leave your city, the economic development office would be trying to figure out how to keep them with tax incentives, infrastructure and the like. If Bob Devin Jones, or your community's version of Bob, were about to move to another city, what could be done about that?

Communities can't respond unless they are cognizant of the significance of these co-creators and acknowledge their importance. In this age where we tout the importance of creative and innovative talent, we need to recognize that the old game of economic development and broad-based talent attraction and retention strategies are insufficient to deal with the select group of co-creators that every community needs.

CONTINUUM OF INFLUENCE

Within that continuum of engagement there is also a continuum of influence regarding the community. At the far left, you might find an angry blogger or community agitator with an ax to grind. They may have some influence, and they play a role. The agitator can often ignite debate, galvanize others to action and occasionally speak truth to power. I have seen one angry blogger almost hold a whole city hostage. In Lexington, Kentucky, I got to know Eric Patrick Marr, the originator of Lexinomics and a prolific blogger. Eric, or "EPM" as most know him, was highly critical of various aspects of the community and he pulled no punches. He angered many people and even threw his hat into their mayoral race, declaring himself a candidate for the office. As a provocateur he was very effective, but it was not until some others in the community began to get in his ear about softening his approach that he started to gain real traction within the community. No one ever questioned his intelligence or his sincere interest in the city; they just did not like his rather brusque approach. Today, he is still a critical voice in the community, but he is an accepted critical voice because of his more diplomatic approach.

EPM represents that extreme end of the continuum where a person might initially appear to be negative or even hostile towards the community. To use the old adage, such apparent hatred is love turned upside down. Lexington–particularly a few key members of that community–recognized that EMP was at heart a passionate fan of the city; he just needed to be heard and brought back around. Not every "hater" can be turned, but the fact that they have strong feelings about a place is significant and, potentially, an asset.

Moving on, we find those that are detached and bored. I believe these groups are harder to influence than any others because they have essentially checked out. There is very little that you can say to this group to make them believe the community is interesting or worth caring about. They don't believe your marketing, and there is nothing you can tell them that matters. For whatever reasons, they don't care. The only thing that can be done is to show them something. Show them an event, a project, a piece of art, something that makes them go "whoa, that is kind of cool." They have to see and feel something different than what they have come to expect from their city. And one event is not going to make them fall in love. But it might move them from being bored to being more neutral. And from there you surprise them again, and maybe move them to being interested and a little curious about what might happen next. In fact, the whole group that is "neutral" towards the city is actually leaning one way or the other; they are moving towards curiosity or boredom, and we either nudge them towards being more engaged in the community or we risk losing them to that terrible indifference.

Charles Landry notes in his talks about developing creative cities, that we don't just become a creative city. The first step towards creativity, he says, is simple curiosity. We start by being curious about something and from there we may become more engaged and potentially moved to action—and ultimately to creation. But that simple notion of being curious, of wanting to see what is down this street or what is behind this door, is a key ingredient to engaging with your city. A curious mind is open to ideas and possibilities. From there, other things become possible.

As we move up the continuum of engagement to those who are engaged and passionate about their community, we see the building levels of influence these people have on the rest of the population. Most of us are looking upstream at those relative few who are passionately engaged and are making things happen. What those folks do has a large influence on how we perceive our community. When the makers are doing cool stuff that we see, engage in and "consume," we appreciate it and we become more engaged with our place. We might even be motivated to try to do something ourselves because we have seen how cool it is when things are made to happen. That may be the ultimate gift that the co-creators provide their communities; they dramatically show the possibility of making things happen and how rewarding it can be to get in the game.

All of us are on this continuum and we may be moved up or down for many reasons. We can be moved by seemingly small and insignificant things. Communities that recognize this can develop strategies and tactics that embrace the idea of how to make the community more interesting, engaging and lovable. These strategies can be layered into existing approaches to community and economic development with relatively little expense. Things that make communities interesting and lovable don't necessarily cost a lot of money. What they do require is insight and sensitivity to the idea that we are building emotional connections with our citizens–not just paving roads, expanding our tax base and collecting garbage.

MOVING PEOPLE UP THE CONTINUUM – THE JOURNEY TOWARDS LOVE

Anyone who has experience with political fundraising or philanthropic giving understands the concept of a continuum of engagement. In fundraising terms, you don't turn a $25 donor into a $1000 donor overnight; you have to move them along, maybe to $50 or $100, before you can even think about asking for $1000 from them–no matter how important the candidate or cause. Along the way, the donor becomes more educated, more engaged in the political or social process and, hopefully, more committed.

The same is true in community involvement. As we move upwards on the continuum of engagement, we increasingly have impact upon our environment, our community. As we become more emotionally engaged in our place, the more important, the more connected and the more meaningful the output of that relationship becomes–sometimes intentionally, sometimes merely as a byproduct of our engagement. For example, if we create a new music festival, we don't think of it as a social capital generating, love inducing, economically impactful, creative class attracting event. We think of it as something wildly cool that we are excited to do! We are producing fun, by making something that is interesting and meaningful to us.

While I am sure that someone who is neutral, bored or perhaps even negative about their community is capable of creating a music festival (or the like), I submit that the more engaged you are with your place, the further along that continuum of engagement you are, the more likely you will contribute something, share something or create something that will add to the community.

Change agents and community champions are found down that pathway of engagement. Often these people did not intend to become activists; they simply found themselves stimulated to do something and were comfortable and confident enough to act, and the reward for action was not money but the chance to do something meaningful. For generations we have thought of people as being motivated by financial gain, but we are now beginning to rethink those motivations and accept that people are moved by far more than just money.

CHASING MEANING

Economists and demographers point out that talent typically flows to where it is valued most—hence the pull of mega-regions and major cities. These places can pay the most for the skills needed to build their economies. One need only look at professional sports to see vivid examples of this principle. Rich teams such as the New York Yankees and Boston Red Sox can outspend their opponents, and most every year they field winning teams that contend for titles. Yet if money alone were the determinant, then every year the Yankees, the Dallas Cowboys, the Los Angeles Lakers and Chelsea FC would win their respective titles. Clearly this is not the case.

In their brilliant book, *Soccernomics*, authors Simon Kuper & Stefan Syymanski talk about why soccer came to prominence in poor, non-capital cities over rich, capital cities that clearly had more money and resources. They point out that soccer rose to prominence where it meant more, especially in rapidly industrializing cities such as Manchester, Turin, Milan, Istanbul and Barcelona. In capital cities such as London or Rome, soccer competed with many other forms of sport and entertainment, but in the industrial north of England or Italy, soccer was the sport, the pastime. Passionate communities attracted passionate players, coaches and owners, and they created cultures and traditions that have carried on even today.

Not everyone makes decisions based on where they can make the most money. Premier athletes want to win—they want championships and they want history. They want meaning. Two recent sports examples are Joe Mauer and LeBron James. In 2010 the Minnesota Twins spent more money than they ever had before to keep hometown hero Joe Maurer in Minnesota. Why? Because he meant more to them than simply being an exceptionally talented player. Mauer must have recognized this relationship because by every estimation he would have made even more had he declared free agency the following year and got the Yankees and Red Sox into a bidding war. Mauer stayed in Minnesota, where he was born, where his family resides, where he is the favored son in the eyes of the state.

And there is the opposite as well. In July 2010, LeBron James, a native of Northeast Ohio, announced he was leaving Cleveland and "taking his talent to South Beach" to play for the Miami Heat. His decision broke the hearts of Cleveland sports fans and angered many around the country (about the only ones not disheartened by the move were the folks in Miami). People reacted negatively to James' departure because we all want our home teams and home towns to succeed, and his leaving of Cleveland left an ache that many cities have felt as they lose their local talent to star cities. James will most likely win championships in Miami, but I suspect that they will not be as meaningful to him or to Miami as even single championship would have meant in Cleveland.

If we rethink how we value talent, and if it is not just in pure monetary terms (or winning championships) but in terms of meaning and personal satisfaction, then we might make decisions that are not financially motivated. When I interviewed Richard Florida he noted "The way people build purpose and meaning is through their work. The work we do is not just about making things in a factory, or making things in a software company or in an art gallery, it is about making the neighborhoods and communities we live in better, more holistic and more purposeful. That is what people are looking for and they are going to find places that allow them to do that and if they can't do it there, they will move."

In this equation, smaller places may actually have an advantage. If the goal is to make a difference, to make meaning and to make a dollar, then you may be better served by going to a secondary or tertiary city where your efforts will mean more to that community.

It is a truism that talent flows to where it is valued most. The difference today is that we need to measure not just the monetary aspects of that talent flow but the esoteric and emotional values. I believe we are moving to a time where people will chase meaning the way they used to chase stock options and bonuses. What we seek, when our core needs have been met, is meaning: meaningful work, meaningful play and meaningful connections with other people.

In Chapter Two, we discussed a new hierarchy of city aspirations beyond merely being functional and safe. I believe that we can amend that hierarchy even further by adding a higher level that would no doubt please Maslow whose hierarchy of human needs posits that once their basic needs (safety, food) are met, people passionately pursue love and self-actualization. In this new city hierarchy, meaning now becomes that higher aspiration for people in their communities.

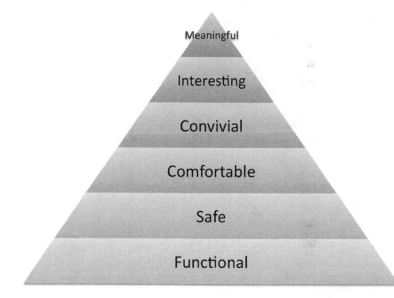

Things like safety and money still matter, but for the creative class Richard Florida describes, and for emerging young professionals, that these basic requirements will be met is a given–therefore it feels like they matter less. Even baby boomers who had their retirements derailed by the financial crisis are still searching for meaning while they rebuild their 401Ks. The next generation, the Millennials, are emerging and joining the workforce, and as group they are highly motivated towards self-actualization and meaningful work.

The winners in this new game will be those places where one can plug in and make a difference, and not just collect a fat paycheck.

A MEANINGFUL PLACE

Cities don't make meaning per se, but they are the ecosystem in which we operate. Cities can make an environment that is more hospitable to making meaning; they can ignore such opportunities; or, worst of all, they can squelch the desire to make meaning.

Richard Florida relates a conversation he had with Jane Jacobs, the author of *The Death and Live of Great American Cities*. She told him "that every place has people that want to find meaning and purpose and use their creative initiative and talents to make a difference in their lives, in their friends and families' lives, in their city's life. The problem is that too many of these cities have been run by or colored by squelchers." By squelchers, she means those who say "no" and would prefer control and predictability to the open possibility of something new and different. Beware those who would prefer to impose their notion of meaning on you, and beware those that would sanitize and "child proof" your city to that point where all the rough edges have been ground down to nothing.

Meaning is, in part, making a difference in the community by our efforts. When places are able to provide demonstrable feedback to those efforts, creators get that all important affirmation that their work is having an impact.

Smaller cities seem to be meaning-rich because they provide more immediate feedback on our efforts to make a difference. In larger cities, the same efforts can go unnoticed because of the corresponding scale and volume of the community. This can be hugely discouraging. Kim Huston, author of *Small Town Sexy* and head of economic development for Bardstown, KY, (population 10,374) sums it up best - "You can live a big life in a small town," she says.[26] Gallup's Soul of the Community survey confirms this– it noted that smaller cities were more likely to generate passion and loyalty than larger cities.[27]

Phil Holoubek is a 40 year-old developer in Lexington, Kentucky. When he relocated there 10 years ago, he wanted to connect with other young professionals in the area, but there was no organization at the time that facilitated such connections. Phil and his wife Marnie created LYPA, Lexington Young Professionals Association, and in a matter of months they had a thousand members in the organization. Phil remarks that he started to get the attention of the mayor and other established leaders, which in turn bolstered his desire to engage with his new city. In Lexington, a city of 280,000+ people, this thousand-member group had juice and an immediate legitimacy just based on its numbers. In a larger city, like Chicago, with over 2.8 million residents, he would have had to create an organization of 10,000 people in order to have the same per capita impact. Add to that the simple fact that several other young professional organizations would no doubt have already been in existence in a city like Chicago. In Lexington, Phil was able to plug in, make something happen and see the results in very short order. (I also note that there is a growing coalition in Lexington that is urging Phil to consider running for mayor. That is an open community!) To me, this is a significant competitive advantage for smaller places trying to attract those mission driven, meaning-seeking individuals to their cities.

Hallie Bram is a marketing professional originally from Cleveland, Ohio. She began her career in Boston and spent ten years there. While Boston was good for her career, something was missing. "The longer I was in Boston the harder and harder it was to feel like I could have some stake, some ownership in the progress in the city. It isn't a place where you can as easily make change because it is so established and a lot of the organizations in town, they are trying to do great things, but they are not the most flexible." As a result, Bram returned to Cleveland in 2009 and, with her partner Eric Kogelschatz, has started several projects including TEDx Cleveland.

Teresa Greenlees is a 30-something professional, who lives in New York City and works for one of the major distillery companies in their marketing department. Prior to that, she lived in Chicago and prior to that, Tampa, where she was the founder of Verve, a group of action-minded young professionals who came together for social and cause oriented projects. Since moving to New York, Teresa notes: "all of my creative energy is going into the work that I do."

And when I asked her about creating something in New York, she laughed saying "Do I feel like I need to run out and sign up to volunteer, or join a board, or help drive the conversation, or start an art collective? I actually feel like that's the last thing I need to do. Because I'd be getting in the way of everyone else and their dreams. Like cluttering up the landscape."

She summed up: "Here I'm more content to experience." In New York City, with its density of people, resources, activities and ambition, she is not required to create the city. With the pressures of her job she is, however, required to pour that energy into her work. In Tampa, a place where there was room to create and many needs, Teresa was a co-creator. She started things and helped make a difference in the city. Does this mean that Tampa is a more meaningful place than New York City?

Of course not. But if you are part of that small group of do-it-yourself city-makers, a smaller city like Tampa or Cleveland or Lexington offers something that larger places do not - a place at the table and an opportunity to make a difference.

BIG CITIES & SUPER MODELS

This does beg the question of whether some cities are too big to need our love. It is easy for us to fall in love with London, NYC, Tokyo, etc. They are magnificent. With them, you have the world at your fingertips—the entire spectrum of humanity at your call. It is easy to love that situation, especially if you like being a consumer (of culture, of money, of life). It's like falling in love with a super model. We become mesmerized and intoxicated with their beauty. In them, we hope to see a reflection of ourselves. Their beauty, their halo is somehow transferred to us by their proximity. Psychologists have a term for this – "BIRGing" or "basking in reflected glory." This often applies to sports fans who jump on board the team du jour.

Fans of star cities can be like fair weather sports fans. They fall in love easily with the trendy spot or city on the latest "hot" list. But when one falls into love easily, one often falls out of love just as easily. Or more likely, we will simply fall in love with the next hot team, trendy city or pretty face.

And the key question about our glamorous, successful, beautiful city/team/girlfriend: Do they love us back? With so many suitors, so much attention heaped upon the beautiful, do they really need us? Will they notice one less lover in a long line of potential suitors? I think not. And where is the challenge? Richard Florida told me a story about a friend of his from Providence, RI. His friend told him he could live anywhere but he chose Providence over more obvious choices like San Francisco, Austin, Seattle or New York. Those cities were "basically done" and it was "no fun to take a 9.5 and make it a 10."

I had an interesting experience in Lexington, KY after I had wrapped up the Creative Cities Summit there in April 2009. My partner Michelle Royal and I decided to spend part of the summer in Lexington and told a few friends up there. The next day I got a call from then Mayor Jim Newberry welcoming me to the community for the summer. We had worked with the mayor's office for the Summit and had a good relationship with them, but I admit that it was a very nice feeling to have the mayor make that call. But Superstar cities such as NYC and London reserve their love for a select few. They do not do this maliciously; rather it is simply a matter of size and noise. With so many voices and cries out there, there is little room for the intimate conversation that might lead to a true relationship. Mayor Bloomberg can't make all those calls! And those select few who are noticed are most likely to be stars in their own right; political, cultural or sporting giants worthy of that mega city's love. It is the old adage about why rock stars date super models: Because they can.

IS YOUR CITY MEANING-RICH?

For a decade now, economic developers, mayors and planners have been trying to create amenity rich destinations to attract creative/innovative human capital. I suggest that we all start asking the question "Is our city meaning-rich?" Is it a playground for folks to experiment? Is it the kind of city you can move to, get engaged and in 5 or 10 years run for Mayor? Is it the kind of city that has a "do-it-yourself" aspect that allows you to be a co-creator if the urge and inclination were to strike? Amenity-rich is not the same as meaning-rich and ideally, places that can couple these assets present a compelling case for themselves. New cities or new communities are often blank slates that allow for builders and co-creators to have a stake in development. But new cities also lack history, character, established assets like old buildings, traditions and narratives; the creative amenities from which the co-creator can draw upon.

Some cities have become meaning-rich by literally having the bottom fall out for them. When a city bottoms out for whatever reason, the actions following that crisis become far more meaningful. In New Orleans today, residents say that they are literally rebuilding everything– which means every job, every project has meaning. For those who are looking for meaning, there is no city in America that is more exciting.

Dan Favre, 28, runs the Gulf Coast Restoration Network, which is replanting trees throughout the area. He notes that for "the satisfaction of being a 20-something who can truly play a meaningful role in the rebuilding of a great American city, there's no place like New Orleans."[28]

Kate Daughdrill is a 25-year-old, self-described student/artist/waitress from Detroit, and is one of the founders of Soup, a grassroots funding project (see Chapter Eight). She sagely noted that "Love arises out of necessity. Out of the sense that you were needed." In Detroit, there is a lot of necessity, and in a city aching for positive news, even small successes can make co-creators into local heroes.

Noted one business owner to the New York Times: "Open a business anywhere else, and no one will notice. Open it in Detroit and everyone talks about it."[29]

Phillip Cooley is a Michigan native who returned to Detroit in his late 20s after living in New York City and Europe. In Detroit he was able to buy a building in the challenged Cork Town area of the city, rehab it with the help of some friends and his own sweat, and open one of the hottest restaurants in town:

Slows Bar B Q. Normally opening a restaurant does not make you a community champion, but how he did it and where he did it have made Cooley into a poster child for the creative class in Detroit. He has been featured in the New York Times, Wall Street Journal, BusinessWeek, Bon Apetit and on the Food TV Network as an urban pioneer and exemplar of the resilience of the city.

"I'm fine with that responsibility. I didn't do anything great. It was a normal thing to do to open up a restaurant. . It's really about just saying, 'This is where I want to do it.' And I don't know why anyone wouldn't want to do it here. You have less competition. You have lower barriers to entry. You have a community that supports you. People talk. The word of mouth here is incredible," said Cooley. Cooley was surprisingly self-deprecating when I interviewed him. He does not see himself or what he does as special and that is what makes him such a genuine champion for the city and a fantastic role model.

"It is really exciting when people can see a young person like myself, who doesn't have a tremendous pedigree, who didn't have a ton of resources, isn't incredibly bright. I hope we encourage people to jump in and give it a shot, definitely."

Detroit's Phil Cooley outside Slows Bar B Q Restaurant

Every community has the opportunity to create meaning. Smart communities should recognize that beyond the official actors, there are a significant number of citizen actors who make up an untapped resource for community change. Some are already fully engaged while many others just need some encouragement, a push towards love, to turn their emotional connections to the city– and their intrinsic desire to make their work, their place and their lives meaningful–into tangible action.

Chapter Five
What Makes Cities Lovable?
aka "What do we love?
What do we hate?"

I have been asking people what they love about their places for years now. It is a simple question that often elicits a smile, followed by a furrowed brow as people try to articulate a complex relationship that is not typically dissected or examined. When they do respond, they start out with broad generalizations about their place – the physical beauty, the people, the weather, the openness of the place. But as they think on the subject, their answers become more personal, more intimate and more localized. What I ultimately find is that it is easy to say that we love or hate something because we have diluted those words over time by their casual application to things not worthy of our love (or our hate) such as toothpaste, light beer or a cellular telephone carrier.

When I say that I love St. Petersburg or that I hate Tampa (just an example here, Tampa!) what am I really talking about? I don't love all of St. Pete, nor do I hate all of Tampa. I am basing my feelings upon aspects of each community–slivers and shades of each that in turn color the entire community. And that relationship is deeply personal because I am projecting my own preferences, biases and expectations into the experience.

But overall how do we really feel about our cities? I have heard from many thoughtful people over the years and I believe there is a significant difference between that which we love about cities and that which causes us our greatest angst, frustration and even hatred.

What we say we hate about cities tends to be big things. Things like parking, transportation, poorly maintained streets filled with potholes, crime, or the ugly environment. These are big things, things that we often feel little power over. Big things that often take years to resolve or to even see progress upon. These also tend to be things that we expect to work. In that hierarchy of city development, these are the failures of both function and safety. These are big, complex problems that are incredibly expensive to address. Moreover, they are often thankless even when done right. Think about it; no one ever says they love a place because the city fixed parking or filled the damn potholes. At best they will say that parking "doesn't suck quite so bad". That is not love.

What do we love about cities? These tend to be smaller, intimate connections that we make with places. It might be a favorite park, a corner café, a place where you walk your dog, a favorite tree, a street festival or a restaurant.

When Richard Florida was asked what he loved about Toronto, he said it was "Cycling, going for long walks in Toronto's amazing ravine system with my wife Rana or grabbing an espresso."[30] Jimmy Wales, founder of Wikipedia, maintains a residence in St. Petersburg, FL, and when asked about what he loved about St. Pete, he referenced his work with the local homeless coalition as being particularly satisfying.

John Howkins, author of *The Creative Economy* is one of "The Big Three" along with Richard Florida and Charles Landry, when it comes to the ideas of creativity, the economy and our communities. He has a very personal take on the issue. When asked about lovable cities, he noted "they provide me with opportunities to be part of a community and to enjoy myself and discover myself, which is close to my feelings of love." For me, one of the things I truly love about Tampa Bay is that almost every day I see the water.

During my interviews for this project, I continually asked people what they loved about their cities and the answers were almost always simple pleasures such as a particular restaurant or local dish or meaningful things like Wales' project with the homeless. All of these reflect intimate, personal connections to relatively small things that create the conditions for an emotional connection to occur.

People love small intimate things that, in the grand scheme of the city, are very inexpensive yet generate positive feelings, a smile and even the love that we ultimately have for a place. These are the chocolates on the pillow or the heated bathroom floors at a fine hotel– little touches that make for meaningful impressions. Of course, the room has to be clean and the toilet has to work, but you get no love for meeting those standards. Those are expected the way we would expect that parking, crime and potholes would be managed in a city.

FIXING POTHOLES

Fixing potholes is clearly a necessary duty for cities, but fixing potholes is like giving your wife a fire extinguisher for her birthday. Where did that metaphor come from? My friend, Michelle Bauer, one of the founders of Creative Tampa Bay, tells a very funny story about her father, Karl. Her father is a first generation immigrant from Germany who came to the US in the late 50's. He is a practical, logical man – "very German" Michelle would say. One year for his wife's birthday, Karl bought her what he thought was a thoughtful, practical gift. He bought her a fire extinguisher. This is worse than getting socks for Christmas as a kid!

In Karl's mind, the gift was very sincere. It was something that could save her life and perhaps the family home. It showed that he was concerned for her and her wellbeing. Logical, practical, but– unless his wife was on fire at the time– completely wrong! The fire extinguisher did not create good feelings or spark love in his wife despite the logic of the gift. Of course every home should have a fire extinguisher (several in fact) but this is not a "love note," one of those little gestures that is emotionally significant and means far more than it logically should.

For a city, fixing potholes is the functional equivalent of giving your spouse a fire extinguisher. It is logical, practical, and even necessary, but it does nothing to create affection or even gratitude in the minds of the citizens. This is the stuff cities are supposed to do. It is the equivalent of a clean knife and fork in a restaurant. You don't get a good review for clean cutlery– but you can get a negative review for a dirty spoon! These are the minimum threshold issues that restaurants or cities must maintain in order to be viable. But they score no points for this, and it is safe to say that no one ever fell in love with a city because they fixed the potholes.

No one falls in love with a place because of these "maintenance" issues. We fall in love with a place because of some emotional connection; often a small and seemingly insignificant thing that makes us smile, that speaks to our hearts and appeals to our higher nature.

FALLING IN LOVE

What makes places lovable often makes them meaningful. As we noted in Chapter Four, the idea of making meaning is a powerful motivation. Places that can tap into that pinnacle of the experience pyramid will attract those mission-driven, meaning maximizing people who create things. A meaningful experience is far more memorable and emotional than a functional or merely safe experience. We don't remember the workman-like everyday experience but we do remember the fun, the interesting and the meaningful.

If cities simply recognized this simple truth, and began to ask how they can become more lovable with just a tiny allocation of resources, I believe we would see our communities flourish and citizens thrive.

So how do cities become lovable? How do they know if people are falling in love with them? And what cities are in fact loved? To answer these questions we first we consult the 21st century equivalent of the Oracle of Delphi – Google!

THE GOOGLE LOVE/HATE INDEX

My friend Chris Miller of Savannah, Georgia, is one of the most provocative thinkers on communities and economic development that I have ever met. He is the former head of the Creative Coast Initiative in Savannah, a creative industries development program for the city's economic development office. In that capacity, Miller found that many of the traditional measures of economic development had trouble capturing the new economy and the new way that people wanted to live and work. So he started coming up with new tools and new measures to chart progress. One of his most ingenious is the "Google Love/Hate" index.

With over two billion searches every day and an estimated 300 million daily users[31], Google is the closest thing we have to a collective consciousness. Miller wanted to know how people generally felt about Savannah so he typed in two queries; "I love Savannah, GA" and "I hate Savannah, GA" and he simply noted the ratio of love to hate. Then he looked at other cities such as Atlanta and Charleston and was startled to find how dramatically different the results were. Savannah generated a very large love to hate ratio while Atlanta barely had more than a one to one ratio. Charleston did better, but Savannah was ahead of both by leagues. Clearly this is not a scientific or statistically "valid" measure, but something about it feels right.

GOOGLE LOVE/HATE SAMPLES

City	Love	Hate	Ratio to 1
Chicago	1,340,000	54,200	25
San Francisco	288,000	112,000	2.5
Los Angeles	211,000	9,930	21
Cleveland	84,500	118,000	.71
Detroit	166,000	187,000	.88
Pittsburgh	109,000	180,000	.60
Boston	909,000	71,400	13
Portland, OR	125,000	63,900	1.9
Portland, ME	102,000	48,200	2.1
Denver	298,000	69,400	4.3
Tuscon	23,300	12,300	1.9
Miami	605,500	38,400	16
Tampa	41,300	28,200	1.4
Orlando	210,000	94,100	2.2
Savannah	81,200	8,830	9.2
Atlanta	446,000	83,500	5.3
Austin	284,000	64,000	4.4
Dallas	525,000	88,800	5.9

Houston	112,000	397,000	.28
Akron	138,000	1,300	106
St. Louis	85,300	66,800	1.2
Wichita	136,000	2,460	55
Seattle	179,000	7,430	24
Grand Rapids	21,300	803	27
Providence, RI	26,500	6,170	4.3
Milwaukee	274,000	11,800	23
Cambridge, MA	6,850	163	42
Minneapolis	74,600	4,040	18
Newark	125,000	16,100	8
Raleigh, NC	255,000	1,590	160
Philadelphia	88,800	57,400	1.5
Brooklyn	1,020,000	40,000	26
Manhattan	944,000	1,960	482
St. Petersburg, FL*	121,500	3	40,500
Cincinnati	233,000	13,600	17
Lexington, KY	77,200	963	80
Louisville, KY	286,000	42,000	7
New Orleans	997,000	76,600	13
Madison, WI	18,900	3,680	5.1
Albuquerque, NM	141,000	1,780	79
Colorado Springs	283,000	5,660	50
Charlotte, NC	269,000	34,300	7.8
Charleston, SC	104,000	549	189
San Diego	177,000	52,700	3.3

combined results for St. Petersburg and St. Pete

Data compiled July 2010

Note the one city this will not work for is New York due to the long-lived and immensely popular "I Love New York" campaign, which skews the results. But we did include the boroughs of Manhattan and Brooklyn to compare and both score well in the index (particularly Manhattan). In this list, the higher the ratio, the more love to hate. Scores of one (or less) are not good and indicate that many people have some issue or issues with the city. There are also some anomalously high ratios such as for St. Petersburg, FL. Whenever I run these numbers for cities, there are always some strange outliers that generate extreme ratios but those extremes (to date) have always been on the positive or love side. Some cities just have not disappointed a number of people and their ratio reflects that status.

These numbers represent the accumulation of thousands of positive and negative acts that result in the overall impression of love or hate. Because Google is searching everything; from blogs about vacations to photo tags to news reports about cities, as people publish content in the vast public forum that is the Internet, these results really are a macro take on the mood of a city. Some will argue that this is a very imprecise measure, and I agree with that statement. But because of the breadth and randomness it looks at, there is a truth that could not be changed by an ad campaign or a PR stunt. The large numbers involved here are mostly immune to such actions.

One more recent arrival on the social media scene is the ability to "like" a city on Facebook by clicking the button on their profile page. What is significant about this measure is the fact that your "likes" show up on your profile page and others in your network of friends can see what you like. This means that a Facebook like is akin to a public declaration of affection versus an anonymous tirade on why someone hates a particular city.

Here are the top 40 cities ranked according to Facebook "likes" per capita.[32]

Pop. Rank	City	State	Population	# FB Likes	Ratio
60	Pittsburgh	PA	310,037	160,700	1.92
169	Kansas City	KS	142,562	42,328	3.36
12	San Francisco	CA	808,976	211,587	3.82
27	Washington	DC	591,833	152,755	3.87
215	Gainesville	FL	114,916	26,346	4.36
29	Portland	OR	557,706	105,120	5.30
226	Charleston	SC	111,978	18,394	6.08
99	Rochester	NY	206,886	31,896	6.48
259	Murfreesboro	TN	101,753	15,603	6.52
41	Cleveland	OH	433,748	51,659	8.39
43	Miami	FL	413,201	48,668	8.49
53	Tampa	FL	340,882	35,815	9.51
35	Kansas City	MO	480,129	42,338	11.34
40	Omaha	NE	438,646	38,211	11.47
57	Cincinnati	OH	333,336	28,922	11.52
82	Orlando	FL	230,519	19,468	11.84
34	Albuquerque	NM	521,999	40,576	12.86
55	New Orleans	LA	336,644	22,810	14.75
1	New York	NY	8,363,710	559,718	14.94
243	Clearwater	FL	105,774	6,623	15.97
106	Yonkers	NY	201,588	11,851	17.01
14	Indianapolis	IN	798,382	43,494	18.35
273	Wilmington	NC	100,192	5,380	18.62
77	St. Petersburg	FL	245,314	12,724	19.27
181	Savannah	GA	132,410	6,763	19.57
9	San Diego	CA	1,279,329	62,701	20.40
115	Huntington Bch	CA	192,620	7,948	24.23
2	Los Angeles	CA	3,833,995	153,600	24.96
105	Richmond	VA	202,002	7,901	25.56

124	Ft Lauderdale	FL	183,126	7,058	25.94
68	Newark	NJ	278,980	9,971	27.97
42	Virginia Bch	VA	433,746	14,817	29.27
49	Honolulu	HI	374,676	12,662	29.59
21	Boston	MA	620,535	20,720	29.94
171	Hollywood	FL	141,740	4,625	30.64
263	Berkeley	CA	101,371	3,213	31.55
217	Ann Arbor	MI	114,386	3,481	32.86
189	Columbia	SC	127,029	3,857	32.93
161	Paterson	NJ	145,643	4,374	33.29
25	Seattle	WA	598,541	17,692	33.83

Data researched and compiled August 2010.

As I noted with the Love/Hate Index, this list is not meant to represent "hard" statistics for cities but rather to offer a snapshot of feelings about a place that may be useful as a broad indicator of general sentiment. The area of "sentiment analysis," tracking and measuring people's feelings about products and places, is at a very early stage. But in the way we broadly measured a website's success by the gross number of hits it received (and still do), we will come to measure the tone and mood of tweets, texts, status updates and blog posts as key indicators of overall attitudes of people towards products, brands and places. "Likes" of a city are the beginning of the possibility of love, and smart cities will start to track these data over time the way they have tracked unemployment, productivity and business starts. These emerging markers –e.g., Facebook "likes"–help to paint a more complete picture of the community.

Note: Some of the most lovable cities I list and write about don't actually do very well on the Love/Hate table. As I noted above, these measures and proxies are observations of a greater whole. In an anthropological experiment, you look at a whole host of behaviors to understand the subject. As I noted in trying to determine if two people were in love, you would look at a lot of things, no one of them dispositive. So too is the Love/ Hate index. For many cities, I think it is a relevant measure and something that they should note, particularly as it may change and evolve over time. For cities like Detroit, Pittsburgh and Cleveland, cities that I believe are quite lovable, the chart does not tell their complete story. Cities like these have a long history and have seen many disappointments over the years. I believe that the accumulation of those disappointments and accompanying anger is reflected in their poor showing on this chart. These haters are probably fans of these cities who have been beaten down over time and have succumbed to the negative media onslaught these cities have experienced. Again, no one measure will tell us if a place is loved or hated but I felt that these cities required some explanation.

PROXIES FOR LOVE

The Love/Hate index and Facebook's "Like" function look at the totality of our feelings, but if we want to dissect those feelings we need to look for individual acts or representations of our love or hate for our communities. We need proxies for those feelings.

As we have seen in the Gallup Soul of the Community poll, the things that draw us to our communities are aesthetics, social activities and a sense of openness. But these are broad characteristics, akin to saying that your prospective spouse needs to have a sense of humor and a good job. There are many signs and subtleties in determining what love is in our personal lives, and similarly there is no clear answer for our relationships with our communities. In figuring out these proxies for love, I looked for analogs and made some unusual and unexpected connections.

I started with these questions: How does love manifest itself? How does it express itself? What happens to us as we fall in love? In an anthropological experiment, one would look at certain behaviors and markers. Holding hands, kissing and hugging might seem like obvious signs, but we all know that they don't automatically indicate love. Marriage or living together might be markers, but those do not guarantee love either. Taken together though, they seem like a fairly strong indication of love– at least more so than any one, single behavior.

In thinking about this in the context of love for cities, I have looked not only at behaviors but also at proxies for behaviors that have no equivalent in our relationships with our cities. For example, how do you hold hands with your city? How do you marry your city? And how do certain aspects of a city make it more or less lovable? So in thinking about those elements I have come up with some proxies that intuitively feel right. Is any one of them determinative? Probably not, but taken in combination they reveal aspects of our emotional connections with our cities and paint a holistic picture of love (or its absence).

HOLDING HANDS WITH YOUR CITY

Holding hands with another person is a public act of affection. It connects you with that person, and it tells the observing world that you are together. It is often the first step in a relationship. The proxy that seems close to this is the act of wearing a city-themed tee shirt. Sports-themed shirts don't count. Though sports themed apparel is huge business and is clearly related to the city, it seems highly conflated with the sport and the team instead of the city.

What I am talking about is exemplified by the rise of niche retailers who sell city themed t-shirts and apparel such as Rubber City Clothing (Akron), STL Style (St. Louis), Pure Detroit and Detroit Lives (Detroit), CLE Clothing (Cleveland) and Dirty Coast and Fleurty Girl (New Orleans). These purveyors sell shirts that have messages as simple as the local area code, "Made in Detroit" or "New Orleans: Proud to Call it Home," or the ridiculous (and my favorite) "Akron – Where the Weak are Killed and Eaten."

These shirts aren't aimed at tourists. According to Jeff and Randy Vines, the founders of STL Style, "we made it our mission to create a new line of apparel that reflects this seasoned old city as we see it. There are enough t-shirts out there that cater to tourists. STL-Style is all about striking a chord with the natives." For Fleurty Girl founder Lauren Thom, it was about creating a "lifeline for people not here" following Hurrican Katrina. "I knew what it was like to miss this place" she says. She started Fleurty Girl in 2009 out her own desire to wear something that "reminded me of home."

Jeff (left) and Randy Vines in the STL
Style Store; photo courtesy Jeff Vines

And the people who wear these shirts become powerful messengers for their cities. The Vines brothers believe "there's no better way to market a city than to brand it from the inside out and have the people who live there and who are from there be the ultimate ambassadors of the city. If we're not going to instill the virtues of where we live, who will? So it really is a much bigger picture than just a simple t-shirt."

Wearing these shirts is a public display of affection for the city. It declares that you have some relationship with that place. Is it love? Maybe—maybe not. But the point is that it does mean something when you are willing to buy and pull on that shirt.

More photos at www.fortheloveofcities.com.

MARRYING YOUR CITY

If holding hands and wearing a t-shirt is the beginning of a relationship, then the equivalent of marrying your city must be getting a city-themed tattoo! If you are going to permanently mark your body with the city, you must be in love.

In New Orleans, a simple fleur de lis tattoo has actually become passé according to many of the locals I spoke with because they have become so common. But so many people wanted to make a physical connection and a public declaration of their love for New Orleans that they got the mark. One of the more meaningful examples came from Dave Melerine, a young professional in New Orleans and a native of St. Bernard's Parish. He got a tattoo of his "Katrina X," the sigil that the Army placed on houses throughout the area after the hurricane to indicate the condition of the house, number of bodies found, people rescued and the disposition of the structure. You still see them on buildings in the city, but Dave wanted to memorialize his by placing in on his wrist. That is love.

Katie O'Keefe is a 28-year-old web designer and a native of Cleveland. After going away to school and starting her career in New Jersey, she returned to Cleveland in 2009. "I wanted to come back and make a difference in my city...in the end, Cleveland is my true love."[33] She began marking that love with a series of tattoos. Her ink includes an ambitious tattoo which covers her left arm with the Cleveland skyline, the word "Cleveland" on her left inner forearm and "216", Cleveland's area code, behind her ear. Katie is committed! (For a great photo of Katie that I could not get the rights to use, go here: http://bit.ly/marryingcity)

Tattoos, like marriage, are not technically permanent, but they are difficult and expensive to get out of. Look around and see if there are city tattoos out there. If you see your citizens with city-themed tattoos, that might indicate a love affair. Perhaps the tattoos are more like an over the top romantic gesture than marriage, but I cannot remember seeing one Tampa Bay related tattoo in my nearly twenty years here. Yet in a week-long visit to New Orleans in the research phase of this book, I saw more than half a dozen.

And I have to mention LeBron James again. The basketball superstar has numerous tattoos including a large "330" on his right forearm; 330 is the area code for Akron, Ohio, LeBron's birthplace. But that still did not keep him from breaking all of Northeast Ohio's hearts when he left for the Miami Heat in the summer of 2010.

More photos at www.fortheloveofcities.com.

A NOTE ABOUT "BREAKING UP"

When most of us "break up" with our city, we simply move. But like LeBron James, Jon Jackson, a thirty something designer from Southern California, had a very visible "break up" with his hometown of Los Angeles in late 2010. Upon taking a job as a creative director on the east coast, Jon, "not wanting to string LA along,[34]" broke up with the city via five 10 x 23 foot billboards. The billboards included the messages: "I love you LA, I'm just not in love with you", "Los Angeles - I think we need to see other cities" and "Don't worry it's not you LA, it's me". When I asked him why he was leaving, he said it was no specific failure by LA but rather the new opportunity to try something different and "more interesting" in New York.

Photo courtesy of Jonathan Jackson, www.adiosla.com

In economic development circles we tend to think of people leaving (brain drain) as being the result of some kind of failure or deficiency on the part of the losing city. That is not always the case, and in fact it may be the exception rather than the norm. People change and evolve. It happens in our personal relationships and it certainly happens in our relationships with our cities. Jackson's creative and good natured-goodbye actually serves as a powerful reminder for us all to think about the relationship we have with our city and to perhaps do something to improve it.

GETTING COMFORTABLE IN THIRD SPACES

Comfort is clearly part of a loving relationship. We want to be comfortable in love– to be able to relax and just be ourselves. When we start getting comfortable, we are usually in a relationship.

In our cities, places to sit and people watch, or simply rest your feet, are undervalued for the crucial role they play in our affection for places. To measure comfort, one might look at parks and civic gathering spaces, but these are often weather dependent.

In our cities, the quintessential third space (not home, not work) remains the coffee shop. From Starbucks to the most un-corporate espresso house, the local coffee shop is where we go to meet people, to read, to get online, to sit and to people watch. It is also where we go to write books! As I write this line, I am sitting in Kahwa Coffee in downtown St. Pete on a comfortable couch, surrounded by a dozen other folks with their laptops open.

The arrival of a coffee shop in a neighborhood is often seen as a marker of progress and regeneration. I recall a few years ago when downtown Clearwater, Florida got a Starbucks – it was a big deal. It signaled the arrival of a downtown culture. When the second coffee shop opens up, you know things are moving along.

Starbucks is often cast as the corporate villain in the debate about local coffee shops. Love them or hate them, evidence shows that where Starbucks comes, other coffee shops actually thrive. Why? For many people, Starbucks is an entry point to coffee culture. What Starbucks has done is to expand the market of coffee culture and third spaces. This has created room for others to join the competition to fill that emerging need.

In economic development circles, the arrival of Starbucks is a development coup and a mark of progress the way a premium super market or a bank office indicates positive growth. In St.

Petersburg, Starbucks has opened three stores within a few blocks of my home. And in the past two years, we have seen several other, non-chain shops open as well. The coffee shop is one of the most visible indicators of progress and a reminder that we want our places to be comfortable.

LET'S TALK: COMMUNICATIONS & SOCIAL MEDIA

Good relationships usually require good communications between the parties. When you are calling/texting/emailing your significant other 10 times a day, you know you are in a relationship. (When they don't return your text, that can be trouble!) In cities, we ask: Are we talking to each other? We could look at newspapers, which historically have been the platform for community dialog. Until recently, every community had a paper, some more than one because they were profitable. Today that is not the case, and while newspapers, the alternative press and hyper local publications continue to play a role, their era of preeminence is passing.

Moving forward, the measure of whether we are talking to each other is social media. Facebook, MySpace, Twitter, Foursquare, Yelp and dozens of others fight for our eyeballs and thumbs. Social media is becoming how we communicate and interact with each other. And measuring social media volume in a community may be a blunt tool, but it is illustrative.

Some of the social media platforms are so new that they cannot yet provide detailed data on regional usage. Most would agree that Facebook has emerged as the leader in social media with over 500 million active users spending over 500 billion minutes per month on the platform. Moreover, many of the other social media outlets allow you to tie into your Facebook account to update your status (Twitter, Four Square, etc) making Facebook the defacto "hub' of the social media universe.

Using Facebook as the basis for the measure, I looked at how many estimated people FB reaches in distinct cities. I used their advertising targeting system to extract the estimated numbers of people "reached." The concept of reach is not unique to Facebook. It is a concept associated with other types of media that have tried to measure the numbers of people potentially reached by their service. Television, newspapers, magazines, etc all use some version of this to measure the theoretical number of people they might reach. For this measure I took Facebook's reach number for specific cities and linked that to the city's population to get an estimated percentage of people connected via social media. The higher the percentage, the more people using Facebook/social media and theoretically, the more communications going on.

FACEBOOK PER CAPITA USAGE

Pop. Rank	City	State	Population	FB "Reach"	FB to Pop.
252	Fairfield	CA	103,683	2,201,800	21.23
261	Richardson	TX	101,589	752,920	7.41
33	Atlanta	GA	537,958	2,924,240	5.43
98	Irvine	CA	207,500	1,009,260	4.86
126	Salt Lake City	UT	181,698	777,480	4.27
53	Tampa	FL	340,882	1,344,740	3.94
43	Miami	FL	413,201	1,532,820	3.70
102	Fremont	CA	202,867	687,840	3.39
27	Washington	DC	591,833	1,759,260	2.97
189	Columbia	SC	127,029	372,100	2.92
68	Newark	NJ	278,980	812,300	2.91
229	Santa Clara	CA	110,200	314,000	2.84

52	St. Louis	MO	354,361	965,620	2.72
131	Fayetteville	NC	174,091	470,140	2.70
47	Minneapolis	MN	382,605	919,040	2.40
25	Seattle	WA	598,541	1,394,880	2.33
132	Jackson	MS	173,861	403,420	2.32
136	Providence	RI	171,557	394,300	2.29
82	Orlando	FL	230,519	518,580	2.24
80	Norfolk	VA	234,220	523,060	2.23
105	Richmond	VA	202,002	413,200	2.04
114	Grand Rapids	MI	193,396	378,780	1.95
57	Cincinnati	OH	333,336	645,220	1.93
257	Pompano Bch	FL	101,943	195,060	1.913
45	Raleigh	NC	392,552	737,940	1.87
141	Santa Clarita	CA	169,500	314,000	1.85
223	Flint	MI	112,900	203,200	1.79
60	Pittsburgh	PA	310,037	547,200	1.76
152	Dayton	OH	154,200	267,780	1.73
118	Little Rock	AR	189,515	324,780	1.71
83	Birmingham	AK	228,798	388,480	1.69
41	Cleveland	OH	433,748	735,520	1.69
195	Bellevue	WA	123,771	204,480	1.65
35	Kansas City	MO	480,129	773,040	1.61
21	Boston	MA	620,535	977,660	1.57
174	Syracuse	NY	138,068	212,900	1.54
24	Denver	CO	598,707	859,460	1.43
220	Lafayette	LA	113,656	161,500	1.42
75	Greensboro	NC	250,642	354,800	1.41
273	Wilmington	NC	100,192	141,180	1.40

Data compiled August 2010

The challenge with this data is that Facebook admits that their targeting tool is very much a work in progress. "Reach" appears to be a function of your stated home town, your current location, geographic tags on photos and events, status updates and mentions, "likes" of geographic places (e.g. liking a city), fans of places, networks of friends, etc. However Facebook does not explain their algorithms. I contacted them regarding a major discrepancy that I noticed when running the data. Tampa (pop. 340,882) has a significant estimated reach with 1,344,740 while St. Petersburg (pop. 245,345), and right across Tampa Bay has a reach of 640. That is clearly an issue!

Facebook responded to my query with the following:

> *Unfortunately, our audience estimation tool is somewhat limited right now. As such, it does not always accurately reflect the true reach of an ad's targeting. Consequently, it sometimes has drastically different numbers for connections targeting from the number of fans and connections that are actually available. Please rest assured that even though this number may be off, in reality the ad will actually be delivered to all of the eligible fans or connections.*
>
> *I apologize for any inconvenience this may cause and we are working to improve this tool.*[35]

For now, their internal tracking data is the closest measure of geographic volume, and while it clearly has limitations, it is worth noting and measuring over time. As the tools become better (because advertisers will demand it) we will be able to better measure regional activity. Like the measures, the science around social media is also still emerging but already indicating some very interesting aspects of their community impact.

The emerging research in the area of "Neuroeconomics" (combination of economics, psychology, biology and neuroscience) has tried to understand love and affection chemically. Studies focus on the hormone Oxytocin, the so-called "cuddle" hormone that is generated in the bonding that occurs in humans, such as between mother and child. In an experiment done for Fast Company magazine[36], Dr. Paul J. Zak from the Claremont Graduate University found that oxytocin levels went up when test subjects used social media (Twitter in the experiment), meaning that we got happier when we used social media. "Your brain interpreted tweeting as if you were directly interacting with people you cared about. E-connection is processed in the brain like an in-person connection," said Dr. Zak.

If this is true, then social media interactions are actually social capital building, particularly amongst the younger users who fully embrace the technology. When we increase our social capital we improve overall measures of health, happiness and economic vitality.

"Social capital" is the term coined by Harvard Professor Robert Putnam in his 2000 book *Bowling Alone*, which made us all acutely aware of our interconnections (or lack thereof) with each other. *Bowling Alone* tracked the decline of such Eisenhower institutions as bowling leagues and Rotary Clubs and the corresponding impact on society. As these institutions declined, so too did our overall levels of social capital: interpersonal connections that, Putnam argued, have immense value in terms of personal health, happiness and economic vitality. Because of Putnam, we now regard our connections with each other as indicators of happiness and community wellness.

Many have decried the Internet as a primary reason for the decline in social capital. Instead of having "real" friends, they say, we have virtual friends. Instead of meeting, we chat or skype. Instead of calling, we tweet or text. To some, this is evidence of the loss of social capital and a cause for concern. Clay Shirky, in his 2008 book, *Here Comes Everybody*, builds upon Putnam's work as he points out that, in part, the lessening of social capital stems from the simple increase in the difficulty of people to get together – so called transaction costs.[37] When we start thinking about the effects of poor urban planning, spreading suburbia and the dominance of car culture in cities, we see that we have traded comfort for convenience, diversity for safety and spontaneity for order. Our own design and policy decisions have made it more difficult for us to connect with each other. Sitting isolated in our cars or walled off in our McMansions, we have inadvertently destroyed generations of social capital development and replaced them with poor substitutes for community.

But Dr. Zak's research as well as a conversation with any teenager seems to point to the fact that connections made through technology are meaningful and build community. For the younger "digital natives" as Clay Shirky calls them, technology-based connections are the norm and something they are very comfortable with.

Thus per capita volume of social media may actually be a strong indicator of social capital and therefore a relevant indicator of the health and happiness of our community. It is certainly worth taking note of now and tracking in the future as the tools to do so improve.

A note about social media: We are at the very beginning of the social media era. Clay Shirky notes that we are seeing the "largest increase in expressive capability in human history."[38] The tools for connecting and becoming a co-creator are becoming very cheap and ubiquitous. Shirky notes that "these tools don't get socially interesting until they get technologically boring."[39]

You can watch groups like Japanese school girls for the latest hot trend or, he explains, watch stay-at-home moms to understand what the really powerful, meaningful and more likely lasting shifts are, since this group has no time for anything that does not materially improve their quality of life.[40]

Right now it seems as if the hipsters and "creative class" elements are the primary users of social media, but that is rapidly changing. I am now friends with my mother on Facebook, and I think she uses it more than I do (Farmville is very addictive!). The real value of social media for communities is just starting to be explored as the late majority of our population begins to join in the conversation.

A Note about wifi: I am a big fan of free and ubiquitous wifi. Whenever I stay at hotels that charge extra for wifi, I am incredibly annoyed. Airports that want to jack you for the wifi the way they jack you for a bottle of water deserve a special place in hell (without water or Internet access). Airports that offer free wifi are among my favorites. (Thank you TPA, LEX, LIT and PIT.) Municipal roll-outs of wifi have met with very limited success. Kudos to those communities that have tried to do it. And if you are one of those few communities that have made municipal wifi work, congratulations, that is certainly a lovable characteristic for you.

A special shout out to the city of Ypsilanti, Michigan, which in true guerilla style created Wireless Ypsi in their downtown using existing internet connectivity in local businesses and a bunch of cheap, easily deployed routers from Meraki Systems. Run as a not-for-profit collective, the project has lit up their downtown at a cost of a few thousand dollars![41]

I fear however that it will be a particularly short-lived competitive advantage for the hearts and minds of your people. Sooner rather than later, someone like Google or the major carriers will figure out how to make wifi truly ubiquitous and (if not free) really, really cheap. In July 2010, Starbucks announced that all of its North American stores will provide free wifi as part of the overall customer experience.[42]

I imagine that community wifi is kind of like how it must have been over a century ago when communities were first electrifying their cities. Initially those cities that had electricity, such as Scranton, PA (called the "Electric City" because it was the first city to have an electric trolley system in 1886) had an advantage in attracting businesses and people. However technology and engineering eventually caught up– making electricity a minimum threshold requirement for successful cities, like sewage systems and public schools. Wifi will go in a similar manner, and it will happen very, very quickly.

FOOD IS LOVE, A.K.A., "CAN SHE COOK?"

Food is love. Just ask any Italian mother. When it comes to cities, the love is found in local restaurants and in locally distinct, authentic cuisine. This is not meant as an attack on chain restaurants (I like Outback Steakhouse, and technically for me it is a local restaurant because it was founded here in Tampa Bay!) but no one ever fell in love with a place because the local Outback has the best food. We go to local restaurants for the unique experience that each one brings; from high-end cuisine to local burger joints, we revel in all of them.

Local specialty foods such as Philly cheese steaks, chicken wings in Buffalo, Cuban sandwiches in Tampa or Primantis in Pittsburgh (a sandwich, usually a hamburger with cole slaw & French fries, between slices of Italian bread) are examples of beloved local fare. None of them is particularly healthy, and they often reflect their working class origins, but each is loved in their community, and they are part of the fabric that makes up the identity of the place. For me, it is a Swenson's Galley Boy hamburger in Akron, Ohio! Just like we love our Mother's spaghetti or our Grandmother's roast beef & Yorkshire pudding, these local specials connect us to the city in a very visceral way.

Pittsburgh's famous Primanti sandwich - photo courtesy of Primanti Bros.

What is the local specialty in your city? And how might it be used to connect your city with its citizens? Some places have already tapped into that connection. Louisville, KY, has been engaged in an ongoing talent attraction program called the "Kentucky Reunion." Sponsored by Greater Louisville, Inc.– the city's combined Chamber of Commerce, CVB & Economic Development organization–the event is actually a job fair and big party designed to lure expatriate Kentuckians back home. GLI uses the alumni lists of the University of Louisville and University of Kentucky to find large pockets of Kentucky expats, and then they bring in charismatic Louisville Mayor Jerry Abramson to host the party. As Abramson said in the summer of 2008 when they hosted the party in Tampa, they are bringing "jobs and Kentucky bourbon" to the party.[43]

For Kentuckians, who know about bourbon the way some folks know about fine wines, this strategy makes a strong emotional appeal to their love of Kentucky. Couple that with nostalgia for home and a job, and you can understand why this program, started in 2003, has been particularly effective.

What is interesting about this program is its audaciousness. All cities are used to the idea of companies being poached and have ways to combat these efforts. What they don't have is the ways and means to counter efforts that go after individual talent. Louisville is taking advantage of this, and I would expect other cities to start doing similar things. The war for talent has become a shooting war, and most of our cities are not prepared to fight that battle. And clearly one of the tactics that will be used in this fight is tapping the strong emotional ties we have with places through the things that trigger those emotional responses– like food, or in this case, bourbon.

Note – I had a chance to meet Mayor Abramson in 2010 as he was on the campaign trail to become the next Lieutenant Governor of Kentucky and asked him if once elected he would take the Reunions to the State level. "Absolutely," he said with a smile. Game on.

SOME LOCAL FOODS WE LOVE

City	Food	Where to find it
Philadelphia, PA	Cheesesteak	Pat's or Geno's
Pittsburgh, PA	Primanti sandwich	Primanti's
Louisville, KY	Hot Brown	The Brown Hotel
Tampa, FL	Cuban sandwich	La Terraceta or Carmine's
Cincinnati, Oh	Cincinnati chili	Skyline or Gold Star

Akron, OH	Car hop hamburgers	Swenson's or Skyway
Madison, WI	Fried cheese curds	Graze or Michael's Frozen Yogurt
Niagra Falls	Steak & cheese	Mari Posa or Viola's
Buffalo	Wings	Anchor Bar
Providence (RI)	Coffee milk	Made with Autocrat coffee syrup
New Orleans	Bananas Foster	Brennan's
New Orleans	Sazerac cocktail	Roosevelt Hotel

SUSTAINING LOVE

When we love something, we want it to be healthy and long-lived, be it our spouse or even a beloved pet. Today healthy cities are becoming green and sustainable cities. Why does green equate with love? Because when we value the environment we treat it with respect, with care and, yes, love. We recognize interconnectedness, and we are willing to do something extra, such as separate our trash or change our driving habits, because we want something better for our community.

Measuring green is not easy. Cities all over the world lay claim to being the most sustainable, greenest, most eco-friendly, etc., city. Chicago makes a case for being the greenest city in America, and it is very convincing. Mayor Daly made the civic commitment to green and added bio fuel fleets, LEED certified buildings, green rooftops and alternative energy sources throughout the city. Perhaps most significantly, he planted over 500,000 trees in the downtown core. Nothing says green in a more visible and persistent manner than a tree. Unfortunately counting trees is not an effective way to measure our green commitment, but counting LEED projects is a shorthand measure of that commitment.

Below is my Top 40 Cities in the "Green Love Index," which measures the number of LEED- certified projects in comparison to population. The numbers of projects come from the US Green Building Council's official registry of projects. Merely counting LEED projects is not a fair assessment because these projects tend to cluster in larger metropolitan areas. Also I recognize that these projects are favored by wealthier communities, which explains the relative dearth of LEED projects in declining Rust Belt cities such as Detroit and Cleveland.

"GREEN LOVE" TOP 40

Pop. Rank	City	State	Population	# LEED	ratio to 1
114	Grand Rapids	MI	193,396	62	3,119
244	Cambridge	MA	105,596	24	4,400
29	Portland	OR	557,706	104	5,363
33	Atlanta	GA	537,958	85	6,329
27	Washington	DC	591,833	89	6,650
25	Seattle	WA	598,541	89	6,725
215	Gainesville	FL	114,916	16	7,182
60	Pittsburgh	PA	310,037	42	7,382
85	Durham	NC	223,284	29	7,699
129	Tempe	AZ	175,523	22	7,978
12	San Francisco	CA	808,976	98	8,255
176	Fort Collins	CO	136,509	16	8,532
195	Bellevue	WA	123,771	14	8,841
96	Arlington	VA	209,969	23	9,129
196	New Haven	CT	123,669	12	10,306
21	Boston	MA	620,535	55	11,282
24	Denver	CO	598,707	52	11,514

98	Irvine	CA	207,500	18	11,528
181	Savannah	GA	132,410	11	12,037
82	Orlando	FL	230,519	18	12,807
126	Salt Lake City	UT	181,698	14	12,978
168	Pasadena	CA	143,080	11	13,007
52	St. Louis	MO	354,361	27	13,124
107	Irving	TX	201,358	15	13,424
189	Columbia	SC	127,029	9	14,114
222	Athens	GA	113,398	8	14,175
217	Ann Arbor	MI	114,386	8	14,298
164	Alexandria	VA	143,885	10	14,389
50	Arlington	TX	374,417	26	14,401
37	Sacramento	CA	463,794	32	14,494
248	Billings	MT	103,994	7	14,856
219	Lansing	MI	113,968	7	16,281
143	Vancouver	WA	163,186	10	16,319
110	Tacoma	WA	197,181	12	16,432
81	Madison	WI	231,916	14	16,565
57	Cincinnati	OH	333,336	20	16,667
118	Little Rock	AR	189,515	11	17,229
99	Rochester	NY	206,886	12	17,241
193	Hartford	CT	124,062	7	17,723
105	Richmond	VA	202,002	11	18,364

Source: LEED Projects & Case Studies Directory, US Green Building Council – Certified Project List as of June 7, 2010

The results were a bit surprising. Green powerhouse cities such as Chicago, Portland and San Francisco do well but, given their relative size, less impressively than others. The cities that fare best tend to be college towns such as Cambridge, MA

(Harvard & MIT), Durham, NC (Duke), Gainesville (Florida), Fort Collins (CSU), Athens (Georgia), Ann Arbor (Michigan), Madison (Wisconsin) and New Haven, CT (Yale). College towns do well on many lists of favorite places due to their economic and educational dynamism, their rich cultural life and their diversity. Richard Florida noted that college towns have shown particular resilience during the economic crash in part because they "are the kind of places that anybody can go. Everybody and anybody… no matter where they are from in the world can have a go. They are a mini version of a big, turbulent city." So it is no surprise to find that they would be among the communities that embrace "green love" and want to express that with LEED projects. But the outright winner and "greenest city" by a fair margin is Grand Rapids, MI. With 62 certified projects as of June 2010, it has more projects than all but five other cities, all of which have several times Grand Rapids' population. Several projects are part of the campuses of the leading furniture manufacturers Steelcase and HermanMiller. Clearly, the culture of the city has become one that embraces green and has created community wide momentum to build green.

GIVING BACK: PHILANTHROPIC LOVE

When you love your community, you are more likely to give something back to it. To measure this, I looked at the incidence of grant making organizations against per capita population as a rough measure. Rather than measure actual dollars gifted (which skews to older and richer cities) I looked at the numbers of grant makers that arise within a city. Numbers of givers indicates larger numbers of people and organizations that want to fund various aspects of their community. Traditionally, many might have donated to the local United Way or Community

Foundation, but as people's desire to impact specific issues or targeted areas has increased, so too have the numbers of grant makers to meet their needs.

"Grant makers" is defined by the Foundation Center, the national nonprofit service organization, recognized as the nation's leading authority on organized philanthropy.[44]

Their database, Foundation Finder, accumulates information on grant makers in the U.S. including private foundations, community foundations, grant making public charities, and corporate giving programs. Below is the listing of the top 40 communities ranked according to numbers of grant makers per capita.

GRANT MAKERS PER CAPITA

City		Population	# Grant Makers	Ratio to 1
Providence	RI	171,557	1326	129
Winston-Salem	NC	217,600	1357	160
Pittsburgh	PA	310,037	1243	249
Milwaukee	WI	604,477	1343	450
Cincinnati	OH	333,336	677	492
St. Louis	MO	354,361	710	499
Cleveland	OH	433,748	865	501
Boston	MA	620,535	1222	508
Richmond	VA	202,002	363	556
Hartford	CT	124,062	214	580
Washington	DC	591,833	1013	584
Orlando	FL	230,519	366	630
Salt Lake City	UT	181,698	283	642
Atlanta	GA	537,958	819	657
Grand Rapids	MI	193,396	279	693

Cambridge	MA	105,596	147	718
San Francisco	CA	808,976	1096	738
Stamford	CT	119,303	159	750
Rochester	MN	100,413	131	767
Birmingham	AL	228,798	298	768
St. Paul	MN	279,590	356	785
Minneapolis	MN	382,605	486	787
Pasadena	CA	143,080	181	790
Seattle	WA	598,541	743	806
Alexandria	VA	143,885	152	947
Miami	FL	413,201	422	979
Lincoln	NE	251,624	256	983
Flint	MI	112,900	113	999
Bellevue	WA	123,771	122	1,015
Berkeley	CA	101,371	98	1,034
Evansville	IN	116,309	109	1,067
Ann Arbor	MI	114,386	107	1,069
Portland	OR	557,706	520	1,073
Charlotte	NC	687,456	639	1,076
Mobile	AL	191,022	176	1,085
Ft Lauderdale	FL	183,126	167	1,097
Dallas	TX	1,279,910	1142	1,121
Scottsdale	AZ	235,371	209	1,126
Honolulu	HI	374,676	331	1,132
Des Moines	IA	197,052	174	1,132

Source: Foundation Center, June 2010

"I LOVE YOU FOR YOUR MIND"

Physical qualities are clearly important in personal relationships and for our relationships with our cities. But strong relationships connect at an intellectual level as well as physical. For cities, the proxy equivalent I relate to loving someone's mind is the presence of independent bookstores. In the age of Amazon.com and giant retailers such as Borders or Barnes & Noble, they are a vanishing breed. But great independent bookstores indicate an active intellectual life and a curious community that values learning. Walk into Kramer's Books just off of Dupont Circle in Washington DC, and you just feel that the community is smart and thinking. If your community has at least one good independent bookstore, that bodes well for your relationship with it. And recall that on the Continuum of Engagement, curiosity is the initial step towards higher levels of engagement with our community.

Another indicator of an active intellectual life is the presence of an alternative media. A healthy alternative media means that the community is not willing to accept one version of the story and that they value diversity of thought. And alternative media means a little adventure, maybe even a little decadence. A little spice to go with life!

YOUNG LOVE

Every community says it wants to be a great place for families and kids. I believe they all genuinely mean it, but I think what they really want is a well-ordered, nice, polite kind of place where kids grow up in some sanitized version of the city. If we want our young people to stay in our communities, we have to start working on that relationship while they are young.

Showing real love for young people, or "young love" in this instance, is about accepting the way tweens, teens and early 20-somethings actually want to behave. Ask a teenager what they want to do and the most common answer is simply to hang out, yet large groups of teens hanging out in cities are treated like a form of bug infestation. There is even a device called

"The Mosquito" that emits a high frequency sound that only young ears can hear, making an unpleasant sound that prevents the young from congregating in certain places. The device is sold in Europe and North America and has been adopted by many cities to curb "anti-social" behavior. It literally treats them like bugs to be brushed away.

Couple this with anti-skate boarding ordinances, teen curfews and draconian noise ordinances that kill live music venues, and one gets a different picture of a community through younger eyes.

So what are the indicators of a lovable city for young people? Certainly, a local music scene is a strong indicator of an active youth culture. No 40-year-old is out there saying they are quitting their job to start a band (damn!). Music is made by and largely consumed by young people. If your community is lacking a local scene, then perhaps there are too many rules on your young people and your culture is too restrictive for them to express themselves. A similar indicator is the presence or absence of skate parks. Young people are told they can't skate board in most places, but then cities don't actually give them a place to ride. Skate parks are looked at by city officials as lawsuits waiting to happen and magnets for spiky haired, low-pants-wearing teens to mass. Putting a skate park into a neighborhood usually elicits the same NIMBY (not in my backyard) reaction as trying to put in a toxic waste dump! Still, many communities have figured out how to make these parks happen and have accepted the risks that go along with actually being a youth-friendly community.

Of course, there are legitimate reasons for the rules and regulations around young people, but remember that successful communities find a balance in that they understand that kids will be kids - their music loud, their fashion sense inexplicable and their desire to hang out with each other unshakable. Those communities that make some room for their needs will create places that are more lovable. If our city constantly tells our kids no, it is small wonder that we struggle to get them to stay once they have reached adulthood.

LOVE FOR THE PARENTS: FAMILY-FRIENDLY LOVE

Every city seems to say that they want to be "family friendly" as they promote themselves to the world at large. Usually they mean that their city is safe with a decent school system. That is certainly important for parents but in addition to that, cities can show love to these parents by making their lives a little better with amenities such as playgrounds, parks, summer programs for kids, public pools or even interesting water fountains that kids can play in on hot summer months. Kids are the users of these facilities and programs, but they are really for the benefit of the parents who are trying to entertain, educate and socialize their kids. Kids play in these areas, but parents love them!

A word of caution…

There is a tendency to try to take the "family friendly" idea too far in a community and sanitize all of the interesting or edgy bits out of it. Cities are like the movies; some parts are "G"-rated, most are "PG," some are "R" or even "X" rated. There is a time, a place and an audience for each of them.

ON A BICYCLE BUILT FOR TWO

For years, various organizations have been tracking the best and worst cities for bicycling. This is for both recreational and transportation-oriented cycling. We have long thought of bicycling as a transportation issue yet in our cosmology of lovable cities, it means even more. Bike friendly cities are by definition more lovable because they are more people oriented than other car oriented cities. "What we find is that those cities dedicated to making bicycling accessible to all populations are cities that have general people-oriented approach many other areas as well," says Mike Lydon, an urban planner & bike advocate from Brooklyn.

Bike friendly cities are more environmentally oriented (see "green love" above). Bike friendly cities have recognized that there is a health benefit when citizens ride, and healthier cities are happier cities. Bike friendly cities remember that riding a bike is fun! As a statement of community values, being a bike friendly, bike oriented community means you are green, healthy and fun– and that is a hugely attractive combination for most.

Cities that are on the "worst places for cyclists" lists have exactly the opposite perception. They are saying that cars matter more than people; that the health and safety of citizens (and kids!) are secondary concerns, and they are even saying they are not a fun city!

Bicycling.com released this list of the most bike-friendly cities in the U.S. in the summer of 2010. "The study surveyed only cities with 100,000 citizens or more, and was based on number of segregated bike lanes and municipal bike racks and bike boulevards, among other factors. Researchers also took into account more qualitative factors like support for a vibrant and diverse bike culture and having smart, savvy bike shops."[45]

Bike Friendly Cities; Source: Bicycling.com, 2010

1. Minneapolis, MN
2. Portland, OR
3. Boulder, CO
4. Seattle, WA
5. Eugene, OR

6. San Francisco
7. Madison, WI
8. New York City
9. Tucson, AZ
10. Chicago, IL
11. Austin, TX
12. Denver, CO
13. Washington, DC
14. Ann Arbor, MI
15. Phoenix/Tempe, AZ
16. Gainesville, FL
17. Albuquerque, NM
18. Colorado Springs, CO
19. Salem, OR
20. Scottsdale, AZ
21. Louisville, KY
22. Chattanooga, TN
23. Long Beach, CA
24. Cary, NC
25. Milwaukee, WI
26. Boston, MA
27. Philadelphia, PA
28. Pittsburgh, PA
29. Charleston, SC
30. Arlington, VA
31. Sioux Falls, SD
32. Boise, ID
33. Kansas City, MO
34. Columbus, OH
35. Tulsa, OK
36. Grand Rapids, MI
37. Billings, MT

38. St. Louis, MO
39. Cleveland, OH
40. Greensboro, NC
41. Lexington/Fayette, KY
42. Omaha, NE
43. Salt Lake City, UT
44. Miami, FL
45. Indianapolis, IN
46. Fargo, ND
47. Anchorage, AK
48. Baltimore, MD
49. Little Rock, AR
50. Rochester, NY

WALKABLE CITIES

One thing that most planners, architects, politicians and citizens generally agree upon is that we need to make our cities more walkable. As with bicycles, a city that is walkable is more people-centric than car-centric. When we walk our city, we experience it at a level and pace that is impossible to do in a car. We connect with our city when we walk; when we drive, we pass through like a tourist. The benefits of walking, from community health to social capital, are well documented, so I will add only a few comments below to consider, but in terms of creating lovable cities, these elements are significant.

Shawn Micallef is the Managing Editor of Yonge Street, a weekly online magazine about growth and development in Toronto. He is also the author of *Stroll*, a walking guide to Toronto that uses the process of psychogeography to understand how our environment influences our attitudes and emotions. Shawn is known for his epic walking tours of the city that include amazing insight about the history and culture of streets. (In 2009, we spent an afternoon exploring the city, and his insights continue to be a core part of my perception of Toronto.) Micallef himself is not from Toronto and when he arrived in 2000, he tells the story that walking was part of his "courtship" with the city.

"When I got here, I realized that 'This is not my city.' And I started walking around Toronto to discover, by going in random directions through the city on Sunday afternoons when I wasn't working or on evening walks, often by myself. But it was sort of like dating the city; awkward at first, getting to know what their background is, what interests them. And it's a thing you would actually do on the first few date, you walk with them" said Micallef.

Walkable cities are also more democratic. As soccer is arguably the most democratic of sports because it needs so little equipment, walking is the most democratic of activities because almost everyone can partake in it. As Teresa Greenlees noted of New York City, the rich and poor, the famous and the anonymous all share the sidewalks of the city. In that capacity, walking unites us and creates a common experience that we share.

Walking also allows for improvisation, a key ingredient in discovery and curiosity. Shawn Micallef notes "When walking you have the least amount of rules governing you. You are at maximum liberty to go whatever direction you want." This type of improvisation is much harder in a car. You may see a new shop as you drive by, but the logistics of pulling off the road, crossing the street, parking, etc., make such random encounters much more difficult.

Improv leads to discovery. And just as we love to discover new things about our partners, discovering new things about our city is a key way to keep the love affair alive and growing.

Encourage more walking in your city and you encourage more interactions, more discovery and more potential for emotional connections.

MOST WALKABLE CITIES

Rank	City	Score	Most Walkable Neighborhoods
1	San Francisco	86	Chinatown, Financial District, Downtown
2	New York	83	Tribeca, Little Italy, Soho
3	Boston	79	Back Bay-Beacon Hill, South End, Fenway-Ken
4	Chicago	76	Loop, Near North Side, Lincoln Park
5	Philadelphia	74	City Center East, City Center West, Riverfront
6	Seattle	72	Pioneer Square, Downtown, First Hill
7	Washington DC	70	Dupont Circle, Logan Circle, Downtown
8	Long Beach	69	Downtown, Belmont Shore, Belmont Heights
9	Los Angeles	67	Mid City West, Downtown, Hollywood
10	Portland	66	Pearl District, Old Town-Chinatown, Downtown
11	Denver	66	Lodo, Golden Triangle, Capitol Hill
12	Baltimore	65	Federal Hill, Fells Point, Inner Harbor
13	Milwaukee	62	Lower East Side, Northpoint, Murray Hill

14	Cleveland	60	Downtown, Ohio City-West Side, Detroit Shore
15	Louisville	58	Central Business District, Limerick, Phoenix Hill
16	San Diego	56	Core, Cortez Hill, Gaslamp Quarter
17	San Jose	55	Buena Vista, Burbank, Rose Garden
18	Las Vegas	55	Meadows Village, Downtown, Rancho Charleston
19	Fresno	54	Central, Fresno-High, Hoover
20	Sacramento	54	Richmond Grove, Downtown, Midtown
21	Albuquerque	53	Downtown, Broadway Central, Raynolds
22	Atlanta	52	Five Points, Poncey-Highland, Sweet Auburn
23	Detroit	52	Downtown, New Center, Midtown
24	Dallas	51	West End Historic District, Oak Lawn, M Street
25	Tucson	51	Iron Horse, El Presidio, Ocotillo Oracle
26	Houston	51	Downtown, Montrose, River Oaks
27	Columbus	50	Weinland Park, Victorian Village, Downtown
28	Phoenix	50	Encanto, Central City, Camelback East
29	Austin	49	Downtown, University of Texas, West Universal
30	Mesa	48	Southwest, West Central, Central

31	El Paso	45	Golden Hills, Houston Park, Manhattan Heights
32	San Antonio	45	Downtown, Five Points, Tobin Hill
33	Fort Worth	45	Downtown, Arlington Heights, TCU-West Cliff
34	Kansas City	44	Old Westport, Country Club Plaza, Plaza Westport
35	Memphis	43	Midtown, Downtown, East Memphis-Colonial Yorkshire
36	Oklahoma City	43	No Zillow info available
37	Indianapolis	42	No Zillow info available
38	Charlotte	39	Cherry, Fourth Ward, Downtown Charlotte
39	Nashville	39	East End, Edgehill, Bellmont Hillsboro
40	Jacksonville	36	Downtown, San Marco, Fairfax

Source: WalkScore.com[46]

RITUAL & TRADITION

Couples and families have traditions. My partner Michelle and I watch *It's a Wonderful Life* on Christmas Eve (not terribly original I know but we look forward to it nonetheless), and we make a date night whenever a new animated film comes out. These "little things" mean something to us. We all take comfort in our rituals. Cities have rituals and traditions, and they are often among the most beloved and authentic aspects of that place. Think of Second Lines (the funeral processionals accompanied by jazz bands) in New Orleans. They can be signature aspects of the community that visitors and locals alike appreciate.

Some examples:

Waterfire in Providence, RI, was created by artist Barnaby Evans in 1994. Wikipedia describes WaterFire as "a free public art installation, a performance work, an urban festival, a civic ritual and a spiritual communal ceremony." Floating braziers filled with cords of wood line the rivers of downtown Providence. At dusk, a gondola lights the wood and the rivers are transformed into ribbons of water and fire. Over 100 braziers light the city, and the atmosphere is magical with a combination of wood smoke, music, shadows and the thousands of people who stroll along the rivers in the firelight. I had the opportunity to partake in a lighting ceremony there in 2005 where we carried torches from city hall down to the river and it was fabulous!

Waterfire in Providence, RI, courtesy Waterfire, photo by Barnaby Evans

Waterfire happens several times a year during the summer and fall. Average attendance is 40,000 people[47], and it is a beloved event for the locals and a fabulous draw for visitors.

Keeneland is the historic horse race facility in Lexington, KY. Founded in 1936, Keeneland is a beautiful facility that is awash with tradition and history. The movie *Sea Biscuit* was filmed there because of its classic appearance. I have heard Keeneland described as the "Augusta National" of horse racing. Twice a year, in April and October, they have their racing seasons, which last three weeks. During that time, the city of Lexington is awash in horse racing, parties and of course gambling. Men will go wearing jackets and ties, ladies in their finest dresses and of course, a hat. It is a genteel tradition that locals look forward to and which thousands from around the nation and the world visit to experience.

On a summer night in Madison, Wisconsin, Union Terrace in the heart of the University of Wisconsin campus is the place to be. The Terrace overlooks Lake Monona, and there you will likely see Mayor Dave Cieslewicz playing cards (Sheepshead, a Wisconsin card game) along with college professors, students and families who all gather there.

For 26 years and counting, Key West has hosted the annual "bed races" on Duval Street. Dubbed the most fun you can have in a bed with your clothes on, the bed race is part race, part parade. Part of the larger Conch Republic Independence Celebration, which marked the "secession" of Key West from the United States in 1982, the bed races are another reason for Key West to party and for tourists to visit.

In McPherson, Kansas (population 13,770), All Schools Day was started in 1914 as a way to celebrate the graduation of McPherson County eighth graders. It now encompasses all students in the area and includes the selection of a King and Queen, a parade and a full day of performances from around the county. On the second Friday in May, it triples the population of McPherson on that day. The entire town shuts down, and businesses treat it as a local holiday.

Dunedin, Florida is a beautiful little community in the northern part of Pinellas County near Clearwater. They started a summer event that has become a community tradition in just six years and a beloved and much anticipated part of the summer. The Wearable Art Show is part fashion show, part performance art, part costume ball, part rock-and-roll show. Local designers and artists strive to outdo each other with the most outrageous, funny or sexy outfits. Models range from actual professionals to local folks who otherwise would never be seen on a runway. The event draws hundreds of people and is a major fundraiser for the Dunedin Fine Art Center.

Photo courtesy Dunedin Fine Art Center, Designs
by Rogerio Martins, Photo by Veckio

In the appropriately named Surfers Paradise along the Gold Coast of Queensland, Australia, the Surfers Paradise Meter

Maids were introduced in 1965 by local business owner Bernie Elsey because the city had installed parking meters along the tourist strip in late 1964. Elsey dressed pretty young women in gold lamé bikinis and tiaras and they walked the area feeding coins into the expired parking meters. They became the unofficial ambassadors of Surfers Paradise and a required photo opportunity for the past 45 years.

And sometimes rituals and traditions are just plain fun and weird! Since 2006, fans of George Romero's classic zombie films have gathered in October at the Monroeville Mall outside of Pittsburgh. The mall served as the location for Romero's classic film *Dawn of the Dead*, and participants gather there in costume for a "zombie walk" called Walk of the Dead. Drawing upon the local significance of the mall and Romero's Pittsburgh connections, they have created a new tradition that draws thousands every October and even spawned World Zombie Day in 2008. The 2006 walk set a then world record for participants in a zombie walk at 894. The record has since been raised to over 8,000 walkers by several other cities vying for the title!

Photo by John Altdorfer, courtesy of Pittsburgh Downtown Partnership

Does your city have a beloved ritual or tradition? Remember: it is never too late to start one!

More local rituals and traditions at www.fortheloveofcities. com.

PLAYFUL LOVE

Loving relationships are often playful relationships. And play is recognized by psychologists and behavioral scientists as an important and fundamental part of our psyche. We need to play! So how do we play with the city? And how does a city play with us?

The best example I know of is in Chicago's fantastic Millennium Park. Two public art pieces are the centerpieces of the park and are probably responsible for more smiles per capita than anything else the city has done. The massive Cloud Gate by Indian-born British artist Anish Kapoor is more popularly known as "The Bean". The stainless steel sculpture reflects the city skyline and the people that surround it. A favorite activity is to take a picture of your own reflection in the piece. It invites you to stare at it, to touch it, to walk around and underneath of it. It inspires you to play with it. The other piece in the park is Crown Fountain by Catalan artist Jaume Plensa. The fountain consists of two fifty-foot towers at opposite ends of a black granite reflecting pool. The towers feature video screens that display multiple images of faces. And the most important features (especially if you are a kid) are the water cannons that spout water out of the video mouths on the towers. During the warm months of the year, the fountain is a place where parents take their kids to get wet and have fun. It is public art that feels more like the local swimming pool or amusement park.

Cloud Gate aka "The Bean" at Millennium Park, Chicago

Looking for an example that does not cost quite so much money but still inspires fun and play? The Street Piano Project (www.streetpianos.com) did not start out as public art. It started out in Sheffield, England, when a piano owner could not get the instrument into his new flat. He left the piano on the street and placed a sign on it inviting people to play. The piano became local favorite as people would stop and play and gather around for impromptu performances. The piano eventually became a national news story in the UK when the local council tried to remove it as an abandoned item.

Taking this idea even further was artist Luke Jerram who started the "Play Me, I'm Yours" project that first placed street pianos in Birmingham, England, in 2008. Since then, the project has spread to cities such as London (where I saw a piano while crossing the Millennium Bridge in 2009), Sao Paolo, Sydney, Bristol, Barcelona and New York City in the summer of 2010. Future cities include Belfast, Cincinnati, San Jose and Grand Rapids.

Done well, public art projects have significant economic benefits for communities. For example, the New York City project, *The Gates* by Christo & Jeanne-Claude in 2005 generated over $254 million in local revenue.[48] Real estate experts cite the increased property values near public art as well as the increased absorption (i.e., purchase) rates of projects with public art. Public art projects are too often thought of as a statue out front of a municipal building, but they can be much more than that. They have become places where we interact with art and each other, places where we smile and places that invite us to play. If your community's idea of public art is an ugly statue in front of a building, I suspect that your city is not nearly playful enough!

Here is my simple test for public art in communities;

1. Is it fun?
2. Does it invite you touch it, climb on it, engage with it? Maybe even skateboard on it?
3. Does it bring people together?
4. Does it make people smile?

Get at least a couple of those elements and I think you are doing well. Tap into all four (like Millennium Park), and you have a home run. For us, the citizens or visitors to a place, playful public art allows us to engage our inner child, play with the city and, hopefully, create a memorable and emotional experience.

More examples of the best and worst of public art at fortheloveofcities.com.

PET LOVE: ARE YOU A DOG FRIENDLY CITY?

People all over the world love their pets and the pet industry is a huge business. In the United States alone, it is a $47 billion a year industry.[49] Many of us dote on our pets the way we would actual children. In fact more households in the US, 63%, have pets versus only 46% have children.[50]

Our relationships with our animals are hugely beneficial to our mental, physical and emotional health. People with pets live longer and have less stress.

I submit that lovable cities are pet-friendly cities, specifically dog-friendly cities. This is not to slight cats, birds, ferrets, fish or even snakes, but the fact is that a dog requires significant modification of our lifestyles and necessitates far more civic resources than any other animal. Simply put, we just don't walk our cats.

Communities benefit from dog owners. People walking their dogs contribute to traffic on our sidewalks, which raises the perception of activity in a neighborhood. Dog walkers are the "eyes on the street" that Jane Jacobs said provided for public safety.

A study from the University of Western Australia[51] found that pet owners scored higher than non-pet owners in key social capital metrics including gaining trust, making connections and helping out neighbors. Dog parks are often among the most used public amenities and are places where social capital is created as we meet our neighbors. Foot traffic in dog parks prevents also the areas where they are located from becoming areas where anti-social or criminal activity congregates.

Washington Post columnist Ezra Klein called dog owners the best citizens and noted:

"My neighborhood isn't the world's best, but nor is it the world's worst. After dark, the streets fill with dog walkers. A couple per block, at least. In the winter, they're the only people on the streets. Without them, the neighborhood would be lot emptier, and the streets would feel a lot more forbidding. Placing a couple of poodles – and my neighborhood has a lot of poodles – on the landscape really does wonders. Developing neighborhoods should give some sort of tax credit for dog ownership."[52]

There are numerous rankings of most pet friendly cities, and all of them look at estimated per capita pet ownership, numbers of vets, pet related retail and the like. However the most comprehensive appears to the Forbes Magazine list[53], which looks at over 20 factors including park space per capita, dog specific parks and cost of veterinary care.

Forbes list:
- Colorado Springs, CO - This city has more than 10,000 acres of public park space, or almost a tenth of an acre for every pet. It also features seven dog parks and 113 veterinarians.
- Portland, OR - Portland has 31 parks dedicated to dogs, the most in the country after New York, and the most per capita by a wide margin.
- Albuquerque, N.M. - 33,000 acres of public parks

Rounding out Forbes' Top 10: Austin, TX, Charlotte, NC, Virginia Beach, VA, Kansas City, MO, St. Louis, MO, Seattle, WA and Denver, CO.

Forbes noted that the list was dominated by medium size cities (median population approx 500,000) because "They're large enough to draw lots of pet shops, vets and public parks, but small enough not to drown out such amenities with overly dense populations."[54] Their top ranked large city was San Diego, California.

Other lists such as DogFriendly.com looked more at the quality of amenities and less at the per capita numbers:

1. San Diego, CA – The best dog beaches anywhere.
2. Portland, OR
3. Austin, TX
4. Northern Virginia
5. San Francisco, CA
6. Boston, MA
7. Orlando, FL
8. Salt Lake City, UT
9. Charleston, SC
10. New York, NY

Honorable Mentions: Anchorage, Chicago, Indianapolis, Minneapolis, San Antonio.

The paradox here is that dogs in cities make for a more human place. We walk more, we meet each other, we see vital street level activity and we feel safer because of it. The pet friendly city (however measured) is a lovable city as it makes for better living for everyone.

NICK NAMES/PET NAMES

We often create a nick name or a pet name for those people we are emotionally connected to. You know you are in a relationship when the pet names come out! They range from the funny to the absurd to the sickeningly sweet, but all are clearly an expression of affinity, affection and perhaps love. In our relationship with cities, we often appropriate this convention—and places that engender such a name have created an emotional connection with their people. Bear in mind that a tagline is very different from a nickname. A tagline is something that you give yourself; it is often aspirational and focuses on some positive aspect of the community that you hope to highlight. A nickname is given to you by friends or loved ones and it goes right to the most obvious, sometimes painful aspects of the person or place. It cuts right through all the bullshit and tells it like it is. If you are a red head, be prepared to become "Ginger" or the obvious "Red". Tall and gangly? Hello "Lurch". Lost a testicle? Be prepared to be called "Sack" (a favorite from the TV show Sons of Anarchy). Or a real life example, my friend Anthony Wright, from Lexington became "Downtown Brown" which riffs on his ordering a "Hot Brown" (see "food is love") one spring day at the Cheapside Restaurant (where they called their hot brown a "Downtown Brown"); the fact that he is African-American; and that he is the director of Economic Development for the City of Lexington and a big part of the resurgence of their downtown. Downtown Brown!

Cities spend an awful lot of time and money on taglines or "positioning statements" that have little or no resonance with the people that actually live there. Yet nicknames that evolve naturally often have the most resonance with locals and visitors alike. Take Detroit – The Motor City. About 10 years ago rapper Eminem came to prominence and, as a native of Detroit, referred to the city as "The D". That caught on in the music community and spread to the young people through out the area. Today several mainstream organizations such as Crain's

Detroit Business and the Detroit Chamber of Commerce refer to "The D" in their publications and marketing. Friends in Detroit tell me that for the truly hip, Detroit is "The 313" – the original area code of the city. Other area codes such as 734, 248 and 586 are for the suburbs and are correspondingly less authentic. And in New Orleans, the previous nicknames of "The Big Easy" and "The City That Care Forgot" seem very inappropriate since Hurricane Katrina.

As a proxy for love, there is really no way to judge the quality of a nickname. If you want to call your significant other "Pooh Bear", far be it from me to judge the quality of the nickname. What is worth noting is whether there is a nick or pet name. Not every person or place engenders a nickname. It might be their personality, their history or even that their name just does not lend itself to a nickname: think "Paul" or "Tampa, Florida". But it is worth noting when places do generate nick and pet names—that phenomenon indicates some affinity and affection that potentially makes a place lovable.

And places like Detroit can use these naturally grown names in their efforts to market and brand their place because it feels more authentic, which resonates with locals and visitors alike.

MOST LOVABLE CITIES IN US

So what are the most "lovable" cities in the US? This less-than-scientific list looks at the above listings, includes interviews and discussions with community residents and the all-important disclaimer of my own "independent research" to come up with the most lovable places. At the least, these communities have come up with a combination of livability and lovability that makes them places that attract and retain talent and are places where we would all be happy to live.

Most Lovable Cities

- San Francisco
- Portland
- Seattle
- Washington DC
- Boston
- Denver
- New York
- Pittsburgh
- Cleveland
- Orlando
- Albuquerque
- Chicago
- Kansas City
- Austin
- Salt Lake City
- Charleston
- Grand Rapids
- Gainesville
- Ann Arbor
- Milwaukee

Star Cities: San Francisco, Portland, Seattle, Washington DC, Boston, New York, Chicago, Austin.

It is no surprise that the "star" cities of the US shine in just about any quantifiable measure of success. These are magnificent cities and high on most every list of most livable/desirable places to live. Their size and density provide them with the characteristics we desire most in our communities: aesthetics, social offerings and openness.

I would equate our relationship with these cities to intense, romantic love. These cities with their fantastic amenities and quality of life make it easy to love them as it is easy to imagine ourselves in love with a stunningly attractive partner.

"New" Cities: Denver, Orlando, Albuquerque, Salt Lake City, Charleston, Gainesville.

I describe these cities as "new" in the sense that they have really come into their own in the past generation as people have migrated away from traditional population centers in the Midwest and Northeast.   As people moved south and west, chasing opportunities, these cities and many others have thrived.   With this influx of people and business has come investment in new infrastructure and amenities, making these cities into regional magnets for talent.

In relationship language, these cities are the fresh and exciting possibilities that new love or new relationships offer.   Like a second marriage they offer a fresh start and it is no surprise that these cities have become magnets for people leaving older cities.

Surprising Cities: Pittsburgh, Cleveland, Kansas City, Grand Rapids, Ann Arbor, Milwaukee.

This is the group that I want to focus on because in many ways, these are surprising cities.   Not typically seen as star cities or on the typical radar, many of these cities have struggled (and continue to struggle) with their legacies and identities in the 21st century.   If the star cities are the classically beautiful, and the "new" cities are the current fashion, then these cities represent that quirky and offbeat choice that is surprisingly delightful.   In the romantic comedy, these are the cities/ characters that we root for and who, despite the odds, find a way to win the hearts of the protagonist.   They are the girl next door, the hooker with the heart of gold and the single mother struggling to make ends meet who finds a way to win the guy's heart after he realizes he wants something more meaningful.

(Or they are the male schlub who gets the beautiful girl in a Judd Apatow film.) These cities speak to our core identity as Americans in ways that we don't often articulate yet are part of our heritage.

Cities like Pittsburgh, Cleveland, Kansas City and Milwaukee epitomize our idea of the "middle class city." As my friend Sarah Szurpicki, founder of GLUE (Great Lakes Urban Exchange) said, these are the cities where "the middle class was dreamt up" and, for the most part, where it was most successfully realized.

America is a country of the middle class. When polled, the vast majority of us self identify as being "middle class." This includes people making six figures to those officially at the poverty level. We resonate with the idea of being comfortably in the middle. As long as we feel like we have a healthy portion of the pie, we don't begrudge those who may have more. In fact we lionize those that have made it big - they are folk heroes. From the early industrialists like Getty and Rockefeller to the modern college dropout turned billionaires such as Bill Gates, Michael Dell and Mark Zuckerberg, we celebrate them because in our hearts we believe that we might be there someday too. We feel like we at least have a shot, no matter who you are, where you were born, your race, creed or color.

During the rise of the US as a global industrial power, these middle class cities and others like them were at the vanguard of our industrial might. They offered vast numbers of people the opportunity to join the middle class without the prerequisites of an advanced education. As the global economy has shifted, these cities have suffered. That once clear pathway to the middle class no longer exists. No city exemplifies this more than Detroit. At the height of its power and glory, Detroit was the industrial engine of the world, turning out the machinery that moved people and armies across the globe. Its factories pulled in every available worker, providing them with good wages and job security. In return, these workers dedicated their lives and their families' lives to their work. Of course a great many people became rich as a result of this growth, but more importantly, a great many people, while not "rich", became wealthy enough to swell the ranks of the middle class to proportions previously unknown.

Many other cities, particularly star cities, no longer feel accessible to the middle class or particularly democratic. As discussed before, star cities such as New York, Washington DC, Boston, San Francisco and Seattle feel very exclusive. If you are college educated with the right skills, they are great cities– but for a society that mostly sees itself as middle class, they can make us feel a bit out of place especially if part of our identity is tied to being able to make a difference in our community.

Middle class cities continue to hold a special place in our hearts and minds. Even people who have never been to them have an emotional reaction to Cleveland, Pittsburgh, Milwaukee and certainly Detroit. A mythology has evolved around them that resonates with our collective middle class sensibility. These are the places where the middle class was dreamt up. These cities continue to feel middle class even as their economies have shifted. In remaining "middle class," they retain those attributes we assign to the middle class: fair, accessible, comfortable, hard working and highly democratic. It is in this spirit that these cities are lovable. They may represent a certain nostalgia for a different time, but they also represent the hope and promise that is embodied in the lovable middle class city.

Chapter Six
Increasing the Love

So many communities have invested in strategies to increase their educated workforce, or to grow their creative class, or to retain their college grads—but few have adopted anything akin to a strategy to grow and sustain the love of their citizens. Our most basic measure of success is their gross numbers: more people + more jobs = growth = good. How can we pay so much attention to talent with these strategies and programs and then ignore the emotional component of the people? Historically we focused on traditional resources like oil and water, or constructs such as our factories and in our shift to the knowledge/creative/innovative economy, we have treated people like these inanimate elements. We have no template for considering the feelings and emotional state of our tools, which is why we need to relate this emerging dynamic to our personal relationships.

If cities did adopt such a strategy, how would it manifest in action? To imagine, we would need to look again at the hierarchy of cities (from Ch. 2) and the continuum of engagement (from Ch. 4) and develop tactics that address the emotional deficits we are trying to improve—the comfort, conviviality, fun, curiosity and passion which ultimately lead to love for one's city. As we move people forward on that continuum of engagement, we create more connected citizens who have an emotional investment in their place–citizens who are the new actors and creators of new organizations and content, who take up various aspects of city making. And last, to make this strategy work, we'll need to take some risks.

So how do we start? The first step is recognizing emotional connection–particularly love–as a natural resource that provides value and fuel for community and economic development.

The second step is recognizing that while emotional connection is akin to a natural resource, it's not like oil, coal, or even water. Instead, like creativity and social capital, emotional connection is self-replicating. That means the more of it you "spend" or use, the more you create. When love for a city is produced, that love in turn inspires and creates more love, nurturing a cycle that feeds itself. Unlike oil or finance capital (which is expended once used) love, as a self-replicating phenomenon, follows rules different from those we are accustomed to.

Third, this natural resource isn't dug out of the ground or extracted from the sea. It comes from us, from people, and we are the most fickle, mobile, emotional and irrational factories of production that ever existed. To mine this resource, it will take new skills and a keen understanding of the human heart. And patience.

HAVE A LOVE ARCHETYPE

In trying for change of any kind, it's useful to have a role model or an exemplar for comparison. In the early 21st century, the old adage "What would Jesus do?" has been appropriated and adapted by forward-thinking businesses into "What would Google do?" Jeff Jarvis' excellent book of the same title, *What Would Google Do?,* examines the company's philosophy and applies Google's principles to other industries, drawing some very interesting hypothetical conclusions. As role models go, Google is an excellent one; from their corporate motto, "Do no evil," to their innovative human capital development, to their amazing capacity for innovation, they are the archetypal innovation-driven company of our time.

But if we're looking for a company whose fans and users demonstrate the intense love and devotion we want to bring to cities, I submit that the best role model is Apple Computer.

Apple has redefined the art of creating desire. Their products premiere like blockbuster movies: eagerly awaited for and greedily consumed. A Steve Jobs press conference is like a rock concert–and Apple products are as much fashion statement as they are cutting-edge technology. Having an Apple store in your city or region is the equivalent of having an IKEA, or a Starbucks ten years ago. Sure, more people use PCs, but far more people will tell you that they love their Macs.

"Apple Love" is that special relationship people have with their iPhones, iPods, iPads and MacBooks. Apple users–and not just the hardcore fans–stand in line for hours to buy new products, and they proudly display them like trophies. They are advocates for Apple when they tell their PC-using friends to get a Mac. They forgive the occasional misstep, like the antenna fiasco on the iPhone 4, because they are loyal. Despite the premium cost and comparative difficulty to purchase–unlike PCs, Apple products can only be bought from Apple Stores, online, or from a comparatively small number of authorized dealers–Apple lovers go the extra mile to own products they love.

How can cities emulate Apple? Here are a few principles:
- Design matters. If you've ever used an iPhone, you know that Apple lives by this principle. Their products are

immediately distinguishable from every other product no matter if it is a phone, computer or MP3 player. Cities, like products, need a distinctive aesthetic identity. The "Soul of the Community" survey (explored in Ch. 1) taught us that great aesthetics is rewarded with increased affection and engagement by our citizens.

• Make it easy to use. Apple products mask their underlying complexity with simple, elegant interfaces. Apple strives to remove buttons, layers of choices and endless screens in favor of simplicity. Cities need to streamline their complexity and give citizens easier access to municipal services. Needless bureaucracy and layers of regulation have accumulated in all of our cities like sediment over time.

• Just be cool—don't tell me you're cool. Nothing says "I'm not cool" like someone who can't stop talking about how hip they are. You can't tell me that you're a cool, hip city. (Not if you want me to believe you, anyway.) Apple manages to get its fans to tell others how cool it is. We know that Apple is incredibly self-conscious of their coolness, but they wear it with an insouciance that makes them seem beyond cool. Cities need to work on acting like that cool, hip city, and let someone else tell me how cool you are.

• Provide great customer service. If you've ever gone to the Genius Bar at an Apple store to get help with your computer, you have seen great customer service in action. Why can't the city's Department of Motor Vehicles or permitting department be like the Genius Bar? Apple and other companies that emphasize customer service recognize that a happy customer is a loyal customer. Cities too often act like they are a monopoly and that the citizen/customer has no other choice. But the very citizens that cities value most, the young, educated and entrepreneurial are the ones most able to vote with their feet and leave for a better gig.

- Little things matter, i.e., pay attention to the details. If you have ever purchased an Apple product, from an iPod to a desktop computer, you have had the experience of unwrapping and opening your purchase for the very first time. The Apple experience begins with the packaging that the product arrives in. Layered into beautifully designed boxes, opening an Apple product is akin to a "Chinese box" with precise pieces that unfold like origami. Cities would do well to remember that the experience of the city begins long before most people arrive at your city center or iconic buildings. Ask how does your city present itself for the first time for someone arriving by plane or car.

Apple pays attention to small functional elements as well. How many times have you tripped over a power cord and toppled your laptop? Most PC power cords have a plug that is inserted into the computer and if jerked, it can pull the computer off a table. Apple makes their power cord a magnetic connector that easily pulls away if tugged. Brilliant. Why didn't someone do this years ago? Probably for the same reason it took over a hundred years to finally put wheels on luggage. We focus so hard on the primary functional piece that we blind ourselves to other possibilities. What if our cities took off the functional blinders and innovated around the small elements that we thought secondary or even tertiary to the main functions?

And most significantly for cities...

- Be a platform. Apple's App Store currently stocks more than 200,000 apps, almost all of them designed by programmers and companies other than Apple. These small programs create the interesting, fun and useful content that makes the experience of the iPhone/iPad/iPod far more than just making calls, sending texts or reading email. Every phone today can do that. Those merely necessary functions are the equivalent of "functional" and "safe" on the hierarchy of city making—they're not enough to inspire love.   As a platform, Apple sets the rules and the requirements, of course–but by making the framework for entrepreneurs and developers to create apps for their platform, Apple has turned the iPhone and iPad into a lightning rod for innovation.   Cities are platforms and, ideally, they should be lightning rods that attract entrepreneurs to build upon them. Some apps reap significant financial rewards, but the vast majority of apps make little or no money.   They are often created by users/members of the community for their own creative enjoyment and pride of authorship; produced by people who want to create something for other users and perhaps be recognized for contributing something to that community.   Cities need to inspire that same spirit of creativity and generosity in order to become that kind of platform that draws in creative, entrepreneurial and innovative people of all kinds.

If cities could engender Apple-like love in their citizens, how much greater would our communities be as a result? Certainly our level of satisfaction with our cities would increase, and our relationships with them would take on new levels of sophistication and complexity.   We would become friends, fans, and co-creators of our cities, and our cities would leverage our talents and enthusiasm in turn.   When you ask a fan to do something for you, she is far more likely to make the effort than someone who feels 'neutral' or 'unengaged.' Cities would do very well to continually ask "What would Apple do?" as they explore solutions to problems both large and small.

INCREASING THE LOVE: LITTLE THINGS MATTER

In trying to increase the love, we need to first recognize that you can't go from zero to love overnight. Love at first sight is a lovely idea, but in reality it is extremely rare (and often quite ephemeral). The better question to ask is how do we move citizens forward on the continuum of engagement. How do we move them from neutral to curious to engaged and ultimately into a state of love?

Heidegger suggests–hey, what's a serious book without a Heidegger reference?–that our moods come neither from inside nor from outside of us, but develop as a result of "being in the world." Perhaps our state of consciousness about the city comes from our "being in the city." Perhaps it emerges from the totality of our experiences in the city–from the large aspects to the small, from our connections with each other, and from many other, unconsciously processed factors. When was the last time you really thought about a sidewalk as you walked on it, even though sidewalks are a fundamental point of experience and connection with cities? As Jane Jacobs said, our urban space "is built up... from many little things... some so small people take them for granted and yet the lack of them takes the flavor out of the city"–things like "different kinds of paving, signs and fireplugs and street lights, white marble stoops."[55] If both Apple and Jane Jacobs are sweating the little things, we would do well to follow their lead.

We tend to think of our cities as being composed of grand elements–buildings, streets, stadiums, etc.–yet Jacobs notes "a metropolitan center comes across to people as a center largely by virtue of its enormous collection of small elements."[56] Richard Florida, who often cites Jacobs as a major influence, adds: "If you believe [in] mega projects, move to China. That's where all the big, industrial mega-projects have gone. Economic development today [e.g., in the U.S. and Canada] is about literally hundreds and thousands of little things that you do slowly and cumulatively at the neighborhood and community level."[57]

We need to shift the scale of our point-of-view because, in tending to see the city at large, we discount the impact that thousands of tiny acts have in the overall vitality of a community. Cites exist in a state of constant flux influenced by the accumulation of positive acts and deficit acts. When a homeowner fixes a broken step, or a pedestrian places trash in a recycling bin–positive act. When someone breaks a window or throws a cigarette butt onto the sidewalk–deficit act. When the tide of deficit acts grows, we see the larger manifestation of those tiny acts in the decline of streets and neighborhoods; the edges begin to fray, and the slow slide towards shabbiness and decay begins. Unchecked, negative acts accumulate and add up to blighted areas that may never bounce back. When positive acts accumulate, the opposite occurs: areas thrive and blossom like well-tended gardens and nurtured children.

Personal relationships exhibit similar dynamics. Relationships are made up of lots of little acts over time. Psychologist Dr. John Gottman suggests that there's even a reliable ratio for expressing this phenomenon. According to his "Marriage Formula," it takes a 5-to-1 ratio of positive acts to negative acts for a relationship to work.[58]

If we map this idea onto cities, we would need five positive experiences for every negative one to make a person's relationship with their community work. In terms of cities, this seems like a tall order. Clearly we have high expectations of our significant others in person-to-person relationships, and so any negative act or gesture in that context has a corresponding impact on our wellbeing. I fear we have far lower expectations of our cities—though I believe our expectations are changing—and that we take negative experiences like traffic jams and aggressive drivers or ugly buildings and billboards as a normal part of experience. Our tolerance to bad relationships with our cities has built up over years of poor service and diminished expectations.

CITY FORMULA

What if the "City Formula" were the reverse of the Marriage Formula? What if one positive act, in the context of city life, made up for multiple negative acts? I don't think it's so far-fetched. We can all relate to having a generally bad day or bad experience and then something positive happens and, like the passing of a rainstorm, the clouds part and the sun shines again. All joys and all negatives are not created equal. Clearly there are degrees of acts (being mugged, for instance, is a far more negative experience than seeing rubbish on the sidewalk), but generally the old adage of one joy dispelling a thousand worries has merit in experiences with cities. Also with years of diminished expectations has come a corresponding increase in surprise and delight when a municipal service does work well, or when we find beauty and comfort in our surroundings. As we improve our cities, though, we need to be aware that we correspondingly raise expectations for our places and, thus, we will have to continue to work to improve those experiences. Apple has set the bar for themselves at an incredibly high level yet they (usually!) meet our correspondingly high expectations of them. Setting our own bar higher—and expecting more from ourselves and our cities would be a good thing, something that challenges us and makes us strive for something beyond safe and functional.

MAKE VALUES VISIBLE (AND PERSISTENT!)

We have seen that Apple makes their values very clear to consumers through great design, great customer service and great experiences.

How can cities portray their values and make themselves more creative, innovative and fun? Make those values more visible!

Take the idea of fun. Cities are not directly responsible for being fun. Certainly they play a huge role in facilitating fun, but ultimately fun comes from the people who live in the community. The city may be a squelcher of that fun, or it can figure out how to nurture, support and maybe even amplify the fun being produced by its citizens.

How can cities help? By recognizing that the city is a venue, a stage, a playground, a canvas, a meeting place and a market, as well as its other more traditional definitions. In order to facilitate the creative endeavors that its citizens have been inspired to bring to life, cities may need to lighten up a bit! Mayor Jacques Wallage of Groningen, Netherlands says, "one of the lessons we learned is that you should accept spontaneous behavior. For example, young people are skating close to the city hall. They make a lot of noise and people get frightened. But I think that when young people are skating in the heart of the city you should be glad".[59]

One example of city going from squelcher to supporter comes from my home base of St. Petersburg, Florida. For many years, the only nightlife in downtown St. Petersburg was an outdoor courtyard that sat at the center of a block of old buildings. Janus Landing was a long-time music destination for bands on their way up or bands on their way down–an outdoor concert venue with a capacity of about 2,000 people. But Janus Landing was (and remains) located just two blocks away from what was the first high rise residential development in St. Petersburg–the Bayfront Tower. Built in 1975, Bayfront Tower had become a bastion of seniors and retirees. Every time there was a concert, they would call the police. In an otherwise quiet (read moribund) downtown, the concerts were the only disturbance.

The long battle between Bayfront Tower and Janus Landing resulted in tightening noise ordinances, lots of fines and a debate in St. Pete as to what the purpose of downtown really was. To this day, the 80+ year old president of the Downtown Homeowners Association thinks that only classical music should be performed outdoors in downtown, but once other clubs & restaurants started to open in the city's core, the overall noise level rose and Janus Landing was no longer the sole culprit. The city also realized that the concerts were bringing people downtown to the new restaurants, shops and residences that were emerging and they started to ease up on the enforcement of the noise ordinances. Bayfront Tower dwellers reluctantly realized they could not fight this rising tide (though they did again raise a fuss about the St. Petersburg Grand Prix when it came to town!) and fun, with its accompanying noise, ultimately won out.

St. Pete also was very smart in hosting First Friday, a monthly block party that started in the mid 1990s, well before the downtown real estate boom of the 2000s. The premise of First Friday is simple: close off a city block, roll in a beer truck and a band. Simple, but effective–the event encouraged downtown businesses that formerly closed by 6 p.m. to remain open late for that one night a month, and people who used to flee to the suburbs at 5 p.m. stayed downtown, for a couple of hours at least. It certainly played a major role in the revitalization of downtown St. Pete that began a decade ago. Today First

Fridays draw thousands downtown, and the party goes well into the night.

How do you show people that your city values fun and creativity? You could start with official actions such as enacting design standards for your downtown or encouraging public art. But those require time and resources that are in short supply these days. An even simpler route may be to just loosen up a bit. The city could encourage busking or street performers; licensing them is fine, just find ways to bring more music and creativity to your streets.

Turn the city into the gallery; it may be as simple as a stupid interpretation of the rules. In Clearwater, Florida, artists cannot place their artwork outside their storefronts because it violates the city sign ordinance! Or figure out ways to encourage positive graffiti , as Toronto has done by designating alleyways and buildings where graffiti artists can create with owners' permission and encouragement. The results are memorable buildings, and visible and persistent reminders of street-level creativity in the city. And sanctioned graffiti actually discourages the "tagging" that cities and property owners despise.

The City of Philadelphia's Mural Arts Program (http://www.muralarts.org) has taken this idea to a whole other level. Started in 1984 by artist Jane Golden, the project now has an annual $7 million budget, has produced over 3000 murals city wide and engages hundreds of artists, students, unemployed workers and even ex-offenders in the making and maintaining of these magnificent pieces. They are visible and persistent reminders to the citizens that the city believes in art, in creativity and fun.

Mural Arts Program, Philadelphia

Whatever value you are trying to project - fun, creativity, or safety, even— that value can be conveyed with a series of visible and persistent reminders. But what values are you currently projecting? Look around and see what your city is declaring to the world. In the absence of a plan to make visible a certain set of values, cities may find their landscapes dominated by generic markers, such as corporate symbols, and unflattering icons like Tampa's infamous strip club, Mons Venus.

Mons Venus, Tampa, FL

If you don't actively shape the symbols and iconography of your community, you may find yourself branded by powerful and perhaps unintentional players – for better or worse.

WATCHING EACH OTHER

We are social creatures. We are powerfully affected by each others' emotions-just look at the impact a smile has on other people: they smile, we smile; they cry and we are sad. And as social creatures we are endlessly fascinated by watching each other. Increase the people watching potential of the city, and you increase fun and overall satisfaction. One of the unintended but beneficial consequences of indoor smoking bans has been that clubs and restaurants have created outdoor areas and pushed patrons outside. Now we see these people and activity outside these places, whereas before we walked by, not knowing what was going on inside. Here's another reason for communities to adopt indoor smoking bans!

Beyond simply observing each other, if we can figure out how to increase potential interactions in our community, great things can happen. When we get people out of their cars, out of their homes and interacting with each other, we increase the possibility of them slamming headlong into an interesting person or idea. A band and a beer truck seem like a good place to start.

As if to underscore this point, as I sit in a downtown St. Pete coffee shop working on this very section, three young, tattooed women in summer clothes, smoking cigarettes and laughing, stroll by the window. When you can see beautiful, cool, different or interesting people just stroll past you, that is a very good thing.

TELLING THE STORY & CHANGING THE NARRATIVE

Cities are a shared story— a common narrative that we identify with and in many cases are shaped by. I say 'story' because, as human beings, we respond to stories more than facts and figures. We remember good stories; we tell them to others. So if we want to increase the love, start with the story that is in place and build from there.

Every place has a narrative. It is the story, legend or stereotype we use as shorthand to define and categorize a place. It is a useful device, but very often such narratives limit our vision of a place— and they can drown out important elements that don't seem to fit within that agreed upon narrative. I live in St. Petersburg, Florida, and the common narratives here are that we are either "God's Waiting Room," because of our large senior population, or a beach vacation destination. There is some truth to both of those narratives; we do skew slightly older than the national average, and we certainly have lots of beaches, hotels and sunshine. But we also have entrepreneurs, artists, great cultural venues and high tech businesses– but those stories play second fiddle to the overpowering narrative of beaches, sunshine, Jimmy Buffet and margaritas.

Narratives are powerful and often deeply entrenched, and changing them can be extremely difficult. Even if you have millions of dollars for advertising and marketing, there is no guarantee that you can change the story. Just think about how many cities are trying to rewrite their stories to reflect their 21st century aspirations.

The gap between the standard, media-generated narrative about a place and the reality of a place really struck me when I visited Detroit in 2007. Touring the region with my friend Karen Gagnon, head of the Michigan Cool Cities Initiative, I saw fantastic pockets of activity, development, creativity and entrepreneurship. I saw smart, innovative and committed people doing some amazing things in the city. "This is Detroit?" I found myself wondering/marveling/asking over and over. I was surprised, because my idea of Detroit had been shaped by the mainstream media– and that narrative was all about job loss, ruination, decay and crime. All those things do, in fact, exist in Detroit, but the other side–the active, growing and creative side– did not get coverage.

During that visit I met the founder of Detroit based Issue Media Group, Paul Schutt. With his partner Brian Boyle, they founded Issue Media Group (IMG) in 2005 and launched their first online publication, Model D Media (www.modeldmedia.

com). Published weekly, the online-only magazine produces about two dozen stories about growth and development and the people who make it happen in the region.

"Traditional media has become obsessed with loss – murder, crime, job loss, scandal. These are the stories that they repeat over and over," Schutt says. "But my friends and I were growing companies, starting businesses, developing properties and the like, and we never got coverage in the newspaper or the business journal. So we thought we would cover that side of the community. We filled that gap in the coverage." Some have confused IMG with a "good news" service but Schutt and Boyle disagree. "We cover growth and development," says Boyle. "That view is certainly more positive, but it is an editorial perspective. You don't read Fast Company magazine to see who is going out of business; you read it to see what's next. We write about what's next."

Their business model is like NPR in that they rely on sponsorship and underwriting by major stakeholders in the community such as economic development organizations, universities, foundations and major employers such as banks and healthcare companies. All of these stakeholders reported similar problems with the established narrative of their city when attracting, retaining and hiring talent. "We ask the stakeholders if they would send a prospective employee or potential corporate relocation to the local newspaper to get a sense of what was going on in the community. They always say 'absolutely not,' which is why we have succeeded," says Schutt.

Though the sponsors underwrite the publication, IMG is careful to draw a bright line between editorial control and sponsor aims–in this sense, they operate much like NPR. "The Kaufmann Foundation gives NPR money and says 'we are interested in stories about entrepreneurship,' but that does not mean they select the stories or have editorial input. They want the issue covered. Our stakeholders want issues like job growth, redevelopment and sustainability covered," says Boyle.

IMG has been very successful in filling a narrative void. In the five plus years since Model D launched, the company has spread to over a dozen cities, including Grand Rapids, Lansing, Ann Arbor, Columbus, Cincinnati, Pittsburgh, Philadelphia, Toronto and Tampa Bay.(After meeting Paul I told him that we had a narrative problem in Tampa Bay and I helped to bring IMG to our market. In November of 2009 they launched 83 Degrees Media.) In each market, a local editor and publisher works with dozens of freelance writers, photographers and videographers to publish about 1500 stories each year. Content is then shared with community stakeholders, who republish the content on their own websites and through social media. This creates an incredible volume of positive content in a community's public sphere. Search for 'economic development' or 'job news' in any of the cities IMG publishes in, and you will find their content everywhere. What can we learn from IMG? The way to change the narrative is not to try to shout down the older narrative but to give people lots of other stuff to talk about – not advertising, not PR, but real stories about real people doing really cool stuff.

An even simpler and more direct approach to changing the narrative comes from Emerging Cleveland, a volunteer project started five years ago by Justin Glanville & Erin Aleman, who were graduate students at Cleveland State University. They started taking newcomers and visiting expats on tours around the city to show them the emerging aspects of Cleveland. "The idea of the tours is to reintroduce people to the city that they think they know, and really focus in on cool things that are happening," says Jeanne Romanoff, who has since joined the group as an organizer. Particularly effective have been the holiday-timed tours when many people are in Cleveland visiting friends and family. Family members often arrange to send their visiting children or siblings on the tours to encourage them to return to Cleveland.

The IMG and Emerging Cleveland examples underscore a key point – every community has great stuff happening that flies below the media radar. We don't necessarily need to produce more stuff; we just need to shine a brighter light on the things that are already going on and celebrate the stories that are happening in the so called "long tail" – the less mainstream, smaller and more localized aspects of the community. This can be done by a company like IMG, or it can evolve out of the informal ranks of the community as individual citizens take social media into previously unknown areas. It can be done by taking people by the hand and introducing them to the city they live in but don't actually know. In this way we can show the hidden vitality, especially the creativity, innovation and fun in the community that used to be spread by word of mouth and now is spread via social networks.

NEW APPROACHES – CITY AS OPEN SOURCE PLATFORM

Danish architect Jan Gehl published his seminal book, *Life Between Buildings*, in 1971. Criticized at the time as being too romantic, Gehl implored cities to take people more into account in their urban planning and design, which had been dominated by mechanistic approaches to design. "I am a people architect, working to humanize cities," says Gehl today.[60] In the past 10 years, he has worked with over 70 cities. His work has focused on making public spaces more people-oriented, which in turn lets people engage with these spaces, creating life and vitality for the city.

Larry Beasley is the founder of Beasley & Associates, an international planning consultancy, and he is the former director of urban planning for Vancouver. He too calls for a more human-centered approach that engages us emotionally in what he calls "experiential design." Under his watch, Vancouver has seen the benefits of investment in the public realm in both economic terms and in people's affection for the city. "Here in Vancouver, where we've paid a lot of attention to the public realm, we've developed a lavish park and waterfront walkway system in our inner city. The land values all around have gone up. The tax results of that have been more than enough to pay for the ongoing maintenance obligations that come with a city embellished with art, and landscape, and flowers, and water, and all those other features that make a city wonderful."[61]

Both Beasley and Gehl are absolutely correct about this relationship between the built environment and our emotional connection to our places. Recall that the Gallup "Soul of the Community" survey lists one of the most important characteristics of the city as aesthetics. Certainly the designs of our cities have suffered from indifference and lack of resources. Government, planners and architects have not been challenged (or allowed) to build emotionally engaging places, yet cities such as Vancouver, that have improved their built environments have seen the benefits socially, culturally and economically.

Beyond the built environment, cities will need to start venturing into areas that may seem strange or beyond the typical scope of their work. Think of the built environment as the "hardware" of the city-a common area of involvement for government, planners and architects. Moving forward they will need to start working on the "software" of the city as well.

We are already seeing this as cities all over the world are trying to become healthier. The "wellness" agenda goes far beyond clean water and air, refuse collection and public transit. Cities are redesigning themselves to become part of the solution that makes for healthier citizens. A generation ago we would not have thought the city played an activist role in the health of its citizens yet clearly now cities are seeing themselves as part of that solution. I believe that a generation from now we will see as commonplace the role of government & planners in areas we are only now starting to explore like sociality, happiness and love. One day it won't seem so strange to us that the planners and architects of buildings and spaces also shape feelings like love and happiness, which are the backbone of a thriving society.

To do this, government officials and planners will need to take on additional roles. In fact, everyone who is part of the city-building process will need to become community engineers, choice architects who influence by subtle persuasion rather than prescription and students of the human heart who engage our emotions as well as our minds. They will need these capabilities to marshal the resource that is their people. People, in the capacity of "urban citizenship[62]," will become independent city builders; armed with new tools, unprecedented connectivity, a desire to make things, and a restless nature that is deeply suspicious about government and often refuses to ask for permission.

The implication for cities is huge. Moving forward, there will be unprecedented numbers of actors and city builders, many of whom will act independent of official oversight and without official sanction. Cities must develop policies to help, rather than hinder these people. Increasing the love means increasing the lovers.

In this emerging reality, the role of the city will be very different from the previous command-and-control model. These citizen builders will need to influenced, cajoled, nudged, tempted, stimulated and inspired, but they cannot and should not be controlled. Larry Beasley suggests that "a city or a government, if it chooses to be, can be a great choreographer of all the diverse, fascinating interests of the city. (In Chicago) Mayor Daly has ... been a choreographer. He's brought a lot of people's energy and activities together into something that is bigger than their own interests."[63]

In a very distant life, I was a modern dancer and fortunate enough to work with some very inspired choreographers. The best of them gave us room as dancers and co-creators to add something to the mix. Rarely did they set movement on us like we were automatons to be programmed, though one former Merce Cunningham dancer came close! Though a beautiful metaphor, the idea of city as choreographer still implies some central authority and cohesive vision which I believe overstates the amount of control that cities will ultimately have.

Cities will become more like "open source" projects that are built by self-directed participants even as they are governed by core principles such as laws, structures such as customs, and procedures and opportunities based on needs and circumstances. Roope Mokka, founder of Demos Helsinki, offers the idea of "wikicities" and notes that such "self-built" cities could make us happier. "There is tons of research into why some people feel happier than others. In all the answers, one thing keeps on coming up: the ability to guide your own life," says Mokka.[64]

He cites Wikipedia as the precursor to open cities: "No one would have believed that millions of ordinary people could work together on an encyclopedia, let alone one that competes with the Encyclopedia Brittanica in reliability and beats it in scale. Then along came Wikipedia. Cities are slower to build, but I believe that in 2050 we will look back and say the same about self-built cities or 'wikicities.'"[65] Notes Richard Florida: "a closed city is a dead city. Open cities thrive."[66]

The economic genius of the open source city, is that it utilizes the resources of the community to build the community. As I have been arguing throughout this book, there is a fundamental shift underway from conventionally planned cities to co-created cities. (This shift has, in fact, been long underway, but rarely recognized in city planning and rarely harnessed as a resource.) In the coming years, cities will, out of both necessity and competitive advantage, increasingly rely on the creative and entrepreneurial capacities of its people. In this new version of the city, citizens who are emotionally engaged, interested in and even in love with the community will be the ones who provide a disproportionate impact on the development of that community. In a world where the key natural resources of a community are dug out of the ground, you don't need to worry if the oil or water likes you. In the emerging creative age, cities need to recognize that their development resources—i.e., their people have feelings and that those feelings play a huge role in people's attachments to place and, most importantly, their willingness to stay or desire to move elsewhere in pursuit of emotional connection.

NEW PLAYERS & NEW ORGANIZATIONS TO INCREASE THE LOVE

In this era of shrinking budgets, government is looking for help from the business sector, from the nonprofit world, from grassroots groups and, more and more, from empowered, networked citizens to step up and fill gaps, to seize opportunities and to make cities better. Simply put, government alone cannot create the vibrant cities we want to live in. In response, we are seeing unprecedented numbers of new players and new types of organizations take positions on the playing field. Rapid forming, social media-driven and technologically savvy, these groups are the increasing "X" factor in community development.

Below, I've listed some examples of the hundreds (thousands, even) of such groups that exist all over the world—groups that have come together out of a shared desire to make the community better, a shared passion and, even, love for their places.

FIRST-GENERATION ORGANIZATIONS

I see these groups as falling into two categories: first and second-generation models. First-generation groups often mirror traditional organizational structures in that they elect officers, record meeting minutes, adopt bylaws, etc., and they have tended to incorporate as nonprofits. In many cases, they were formed before the social media tools we have today, like Facebook and Twitter, were even invented.

Many of these organizations can trace their origins back to Richard Florida's ideas. Whether you agree or disagree with him, Florida's impact on the overall conversation about cities and creativity cannot be disputed. When he published his seminal book, *The Rise of the Creative Class*, in 2002, Florida began barnstorming all over the world with his message about creativity. His powerful talks spawned a number of organizations, which took up his ideas in an effort to realize them in their own communities.

CREATIVE TAMPA BAY (CREATIVETAMPABAY.COM)

Creative Tampa Bay was formed in early 2004 as an all-volunteer, grassroots, nonprofit organization with no offices, no employees, and no budget. It does however have officers, minutes and bylaws. (I served as president of the organization from 2005-07.) Creative Tampa Bay commissioned research projects, engaged speakers on various topics, presented the first Creative Cites Summit, and held various workshops and salons to bring people together in conversation about community, economic, and social development. Though the group never talked directly about love (at events or in meetings), its mission of making a more interesting and vital community aimed to move people upwards on the continuum of engagement. Creative Tampa Bay continues today as a "catalytic" organization that invests occasional resources in projects intended to "change the conversation" in the Tampa Bay area. It has recently made a conscious shift to try to become more like its start up origins and become less formalized.

MICHIGAN COOL CITIES (COOLCITIES.COM)

Inspired by Richard Florida, Michigan Governor Jennifer Granholm created the Cool Cities Initiative in 2003 as a way to kick-start the creative economy in her state. Cool Cities pooled existing resources into a comprehensive community "resource toolbox" that local actors could access. A small amount of money was allocated for grants to communities, provided that they created a local team to work with the state and take local leadership of their projects. Within a year, over 100 Cool Cities teams had formed to act as a local focal point for citizen action and government resource allocation.

In recent years, the Michigan Cool Cities Initiative has been mocked and derided as a "feel good" exercise in marketing and spin. (Perhaps the program's name has something to do with this perception.) Such criticism misses out on the real value of the program. Cool Cities empowered local groups all over Michigan to gather around the idea of making their places better. Networks that would not otherwise have formed were brought together and, amazingly, most of them continue to work together in their communities–years since the funding for Cool Cities ran out. The legacy of Cool Cities lives on in those networks and the small, lovable projects they helped to fund, such as the Community Art Center in Saugatuck (a former supermarket) or the revitalization of the famed Eastern Market in Detroit.

Creative Tampa Bay and Cool Cities represent bookends of the first generation of "creative city" organizations. Creative Tampa Bay exemplifies the grassroots, "bottom up" groups that formed without any official mandate. Cool Cities was one of the few state-sponsored, "top down" approaches to the problem; it represents what government (in partnership with citizens) can do to make more creative, vital, and livable cities.

THE SECOND GENERATION

Consider how much better the second generation of the iPod was than the first, or how the second generation Kindle has more than one-upped its predecessor. Second generation products, services, and groups often make the first generation look like dinosaurs. They build upon first-generation knowledge and success, but they also have the advantage of tools–especially technology–that the first generation never knew. When Creative Tampa Bay and Cool Cities launched, there was no YouTube, no Facebook, no Flickr, no Twitter and no smart phones.

The second-generation groups are more social, more networked and more technologically adept. They are also more issue-oriented, less formal and more democratic than prior groups. Some of them never incorporate or seek official status.

In many cases, they grow out of an existing group of friends or colleagues who decide to get off the bench and do something.

Matt Clayson, Director of the Detroit Creative Corridor Center, described these organizations as "temporary, movement-based groups that form around a common set of ideas and then disintegrate, and then a new group forms around a different set of common ideas." In addition to the Creative Corridor, Matt is also one of the founders of Declare Detroit, an archetypal second-generation organization.

DECLARE DETROIT (DECLAREDETROIT.WORDPRESS. COM)

Declare Detroit began with the drafting of the "Detroit Declaration" by Clayson and twenty friends, who laid out their principles for rebuilding the city. The manifesto outlines their beliefs in the importance of transportation, sustainability, land use, and arts and culture for the region—and it invites others to sign the declaration. When it launched in early 2010, the Detroit Declaration received immediate attention across the nation. (USA Today featured the group in a February article.) Since the launch of the project, more than 4,000 people have signed the document, and 12,000 people have become a fan of the Detroit Declaration on Facebook.

BROKEN CITY LAB (BROKENCITYLAB.ORG)

Broken City Lab describes itself as "an artist-led interdisciplinary creative research group that tactically disrupts and engages the city, its communities, and its infrastructures to re-imagine the potential for action in the collapsing post-industrial city of Windsor, Ontario." An even better description might be found in their unofficial slogan: "Make Things Happen."

Artist and teacher Justin Langlois formed Broken City Lab after a conversation with his fiancé about the failure of large-scale protests in North America, particularly in recent years. What if a protest was smaller in scale, with smaller scale aspirations? Around this idea, Justin recruited artists and the design students he was teaching, and they began a series of disruptive, guerilla-style projects around Windsor. The group made international headlines in November 2009 with their "Cross-Border Communications" project, when over the course of several nights they projected messages directed at the city of Detroit onto the sides of buildings in Windsor. Giant text messages including "Let's Talk," "Can we be friends?," and "Windsor + Detroit = BFF?" became visible across the river in downtown Detroit. The point of the intervention was to underscore how interconnected the two cites are, yet how many barriers exist between them. In true guerrilla fashion, Broken City Lab did not have official permission to do this, and it never dawned on them to ask.

Cross Border Communications - 2009, Photo courtesy of Broken City Lab

Since then, Broken City Lab has been engaged by Windsor to work in conjunction with city government. Most recently they launched "Storefront Residency for Social Innovation," a project for which the city permitted artists and entrepreneurs to occupy a block of empty storefronts for 30 days in July 2010 in an effort to re-imagine what those unused spaces might be capable of becoming.

The Lab remains a loose collective that meets to discuss ideas and opportunities; it has no formal structures and no official leadership.

These second-generation groups and hundreds of others like them are rewriting the definition of community and social engagement. According to Matt Clayson of Declare Detroit "Maybe [this] is the new model because it is so much easier to build movements now with the advent of social media, with the advent of smart phones and new technologies than it was even five years ago when it took a week to get out an email blast."

These groups pop up around networks of friends, leveraging technology and social media to channel their shared desire to make something happen. They may also be far more short-lived than first gen groups; they may dissolve just as quickly as they come together. Maybe that's not a bad thing. "I wouldn't feel bad if in a year Declare Detroit, if we had our wins and were gone and something else is taking it up. I wouldn't feel bad if we had completely new leadership team on board," Clayson says.

To increase the love, cities and "official" organizations need to figure out how to partner and co-exist with these second-generation groups. Just as the major political parties have learned to work with citizen groups, cities need to adjust. As municipal budgets and resources dwindle, it becomes imperative to tap into citizen groups as forces for development.

But such groups exist outside of traditional government control and sanction. As such, they can seem like threateningly random elements in the mix. Cities that can adjust to the challenge of relinquishing some authority in this emerging reality will find scores of eager, passionate and engaged community champions to work with. Alienate those potential champions, and you might face a veritable guerilla army, armed with smart phones and Tweet Deck, who can create far more noise than their numbers would imply. Or worst of all, they may opt to take their talents and enthusiasm elsewhere.

WHAT CAN YOU DO?

So what can you do as an individual? How can you increase the love and rekindle some passion for your hometown? Maybe you aren't ready to go out and start a movement or tattoo "Burbank" across your chest, but there are some simple steps that can help to move the love forward.

Don't be afraid to say "love." Start using the word "love" in discussions about your city. Just saying the word adds a needed emotional element to the conversation. Also, talk is contagious. You hear someone say something or use an interesting phrase and you in turn use it. If you start saying "love" others will pick up on that and may in turn start using it as well.

Role play. Pretend you are a tourist in your own city. Try to see it with fresh eyes and imagine how a newcomer might see the city for the first time. Plan a date with your significant other, go to the tourist spots that locals generally avoid and try to imagine the impression these places make on visitors. Imagine yourself as a recent retiree and see the city from that perspective. If you are older, visit a neighborhood where a recent college grad might choose to live.

Try a new transport mode. Our daily lives are shaped by habits, like the way we travel to work each day. In many ways these habits become our only way of experiencing the city. Of course, it can get boring when you see the same streets or the same signs every day. Change the view! Once a month, just try another mode of transport, such as biking, taking the subway, bus, or walking. The same streets will look very different from the saddle of a bicycle. Take a different route to work, even, so that you might see something new and different.

Try a "three way." Maybe you and your city just need a third party to spice things up. Consider spending a couple of months in another city if your work offers the flexibility. Sites such as HomeExchange.com or HomeLink.org allow you to connect with other people who have houses to swap. My partner, Michelle, and I spent the summer of 2009 in Leeds in the UK; as much as we enjoyed it, we came home with a newfound appreciation for the things in St. Pete we had taken for granted.

Invite friends to your city and play host. In Florida, the long-standing joke is that the only time Floridians go to the beach is when guests from out of town visit. Often, living in a place makes you immune to its charms, as strangers see them. Having guests pushes you to showcase the best and most interesting aspects of your city to them, and it makes you think about your city's best features as the highlights they really are.

Become a co-creator or volunteer to help a project that is already underway. Many people are not ready for the time commitment of creating a new project or organization but would like to join in or volunteer with existing projects. Volunteering is an easy way to engage, and it might entice you into becoming even more engaged as a co-creator.

Use more social media. We are at the dawn of the social media era. Some people may argue about the quality of interaction social media offers, but evidence and simple observation suggests that social media builds social capital. Facebook, Twitter and the like may look and feel different from the classic Kiwanis Club, but they nurture social capital nonetheless.

Chapter Seven
Love Notes

A recurring thread in this book is the notion that small things, though seemingly insignificant, can have disproportionate impacts. As a man I have learned the lesson that little things matter by making the classic rookie mistake, which many men make, of forgetting to get the card with the flowers or the gift. In our ignorance, we think that the flowers or the gift is what matters. Certainly those things do matter, but experience shows us that the card means as much or even more. That seemingly insignificant 'extra' can make or break the experience. And in our relationships with our places, little things– like the card with the gift–can have an outsized impact on our feelings about our cities. Bill Strickland, the inspirational head of Manchester Bidwell Corporation in Pittsburgh, talks about the importance of flowers and sunlight and water fountains in his moving presentation about his work. He talks about having fresh cut flowers in the halls of his training center for the kids and the adults who go there for the after school programs or for the adult education services provided. The center is located in one of the most challenged neighborhoods in Pittsburgh and some would wonder about the importance of fresh flowers and artistic touches but Strickland is undeterred.

"The cost is incidental but the impact is significant," says Strickland. These touches, seemingly extravagant, are at the heart of his strategy. Treat everyone like a world-class citizen and they will respond in kind. These inner city kids and welfare moms deserve to see beauty just as those in the affluent suburbs of the city. Strickland believes that right is expressed through the flowers, the sunlight and the water fountain. They are visible and persistent reminders that everyone should be treated like a world-class citizen. His results are nothing short of miraculous. In over 20 years of operations, Strickland boasts that they have never had an incident of violence or theft at the center and in a community that graduates less than 50% of its kids from high school, nearly 100% of the kids that go through his after school program graduate from high school and most get into college as well. Communities elsewhere are taking note of the success as half a dozen other cities have opened centers based on their formulas, with Strickland's stated goal being a hundred centers in the US and a hundred more worldwide.

In making lovable cities, just as in making loving relationships, little things matter—a lot. Small gestures, tiny in the grand scheme of the city or the relationship, have an outsized impact on the nature and quality of that relationship. They are the chocolate on the pillow and the fresh cut flowers in the hallways. I call them "Love Notes."

A love note is something that endears a place to its residents, something that makes them smile or feel at ease, something that provides them with an emotional connection to their place. Love notes may be big (Millennium Park in Chicago is a love note with a giant bouquet and chocolates— delivered in a new Lexus!) or they may be very small (a pocket-sized park or a great place to sit and watch people). Some are planned and created by cities, some occur organically and some come from the work we, as citizens, do to give a little something back to our beloved city.

Some of my favorite love notes include:

DUPONT CIRCLE – WASHINGTON DC

Dupont Circle is a gem in a gem of a city. The park sits at the intersection of several of the major streets in DC. A huge metro station acts like a giant heart as it takes in people and expels them with each 'beat' of an arriving train. Restaurants and bars abound, and residential homes (prized and, thus, expensive) are located mere steps off the Circle. As I sat there with my friend Rodgers Frantz on an unseasonably warm March afternoon, he remarked, "there's an intimacy to Dupont Circle that I've always loved. And I've always felt, even when I first came here as a student 30 years ago, that Dupont Circle is the heart of Washington— the living, breathing heart of Washington. It's intimate because it's where you go to people watch; it's where you go to be seen by others; it's a place where you sit to rest or sit to think, or, as my father said, 'Sometimes I sit and think and sometimes I just sit.'"

EPIC SMALL- PLANTING FLOWERS IN LEXINGTON, KY

Arising out of the 2010 Creative Cities Summit and the follow-up Unconference "Now What Lexington?," a group of people created a movement that challenged city residents to do small, creative things that would move themselves and the community forward. EpicSmall.com was born. On the site, you declare your small act, set a deadline and then tell the world if you accomplished this act. One of the best examples to come from Epic Small arose out of a collaboration between husband and wife Thomas and Jeorg Sauer, who decided to plant roses at the base of stop signs in their neighborhood— a small, intimate and beautiful little gesture to the city, their neighborhood and to themselves. "Amazingly enough, neither owner of both properties has replanted them, and they get mowed around," says Jeorg Sauer. "I smile each time I look at them."

From left: Ben Self, Rebecca Self, Thomas Sauer and Jeorg Sauer (seven months pregnant!). Photo courtesy of Jeorg Sauer.

ST. PETERSBURG SATURDAY MORNING MARKET

Founded in 2002, this open-air market has grown into the largest single day market in the southeast, with upwards of 10,000 visitors and 120 vendors converging on downtown

St. Pete on Saturdays. People flock to the market to buy organic vegetables, bamboo clothing, hand carved furniture, artisanal cheeses, smoked turkey legs and militant omelets all in one place. (The International People's Democratic Uhuru Movement–better known as the Uhurus–are a political group in St. Petersburg who have, over the years, called for the legal separation of the primarily black south side of St. Petersburg from the city as well as a separate police force for the black community. They set up a tent at the market every Saturday where they serve breakfast, including omelets. Politics aside, it is a really good omelet.) Parents with kids are nearly outnumbered by people with dogs, as the market has become the place where St. Pete goes to meet itself. When he was mayor of St. Petersburg, Rick Baker could often be seen playing his guitar there with various bands–a wonderfully humanizing gesture on his part and something that absolutely endeared him, and the city as a whole, to the people at the market.

Saturday Morning Market, downtown St. Petersburg

NYC - TIMES SQUARE & HIGH LINE PARK

Two of my favorite New York City love notes debuted in 2009: the newly pedestrian friendly Times Square and High Line Park in the Meatpacking District.

New York Mayor Michael Bloomberg and Transportation Commissioner Janette Sadik-Khan began pedestrian-friendly Times Square as an experiment in 2009. The response to their people space, created in the heart of the city, has been overwhelmingly positive. Complete with seating and free wifi, the area invites you to sit, people watch and amble in a way that the old Times Square did not. Sidewalks crowded with tourists and busy locals, surrounded by cars, did not make for a lovable place.

The experiment was made permanent in February 2010. Noted New York Magazine: "It took a bureaucrat's intervention to make the place human again, to clear a little room for leisurely amazement in the lunatic center of this crazed metropolis."[67]

Pedestrian friendly Times Square

HIGH LINE PARK

The High Line is a public park built on a 1.45 mile-long elevated rail structure in Manhattan's Meatpacking District. After the rail line ceased operations in 1980, New Yorkers debated what to do with the remaining structure for nearly 30 years. A group of citizens called Friends of the High Line, which formed in 1999, ultimately saved the structure from demolition and provided the impetus to turn it into an innovative green space for the city. Since the park opened in 2009, it has been heralded as a fantastic example of adaptive reuse of an industrial asset. More than that, it offers a wonderful stroll above the hustle and bustle of the street below and a place for people to see and experience the city in a new way.

High Line Park in Winter

With the success of High Line Park, several other cities–Chicago, Philadelphia and Jersey City– have expressed interest in converting similar tracks into green space[68], and Harlem is pushing to have the next High Line in the New York area.[69]

Despite the cost of these projects, in the grand scheme of New York, they are small expenditures. But it's the small things that create an outsized amount of delight for residents and visitors to the city. They are perfect love notes to the people of New York.

A LOVE LETTER FOR YOU - PHILADELPHIA

Here's a love note that's literally a love note! Conceived by graffiti artist Steve Powers and produced in partnership with the Philadelphia Mural Arts program, the project "A Love Letter for You" (www.aloveletterforyou.com) created an extended "love letter" to the city on 50 walls visible along the Market Street train line. Enlisting 40 local and international artists, the murals depict a message from one lover to another, but they can easily be read as exchanges between any viewer and the city. Messages include loving, smile-inducing sentiments such as "If you were here, I'd be home" and "Your everafter is all I'm after."

Love Letter: If You Were Here, I'd Be Home Now
(c) 2009 City of Philadelphia Mural Arts Program / Steve Powers
Photos by Adam Wallacavage & Sarah Lester

Before the project, Powers had worked underground as an artist, illegally painting many of the walls his love letter project now covers. Recently, the city of Syracuse, NY, commissioned him to do a similar project. The love spreads!

ST. PETERSBURG, FL–DOG PARKS AND PLAYGROUNDS

Rick Baker was mayor of St. Petersburg for two successful terms from 2001 to 2009. During that time he became known for the prodigious number of dog parks and playgrounds the city opened during his tenure (11 new playgrounds and 5 new dog parks). While his commitment to new parks became a bit of a joke locally, Baker proudly said that no child in St. Petersburg should be more than a half-mile away from a playground. The city now boasts 58 playgrounds in total. Playgrounds and dog parks may seem like silly extravagances, but for parents and pet owners (a pretty good constituency, actually) these places made St. Pete a much more lovable city. Baker's effort created more third spaces where people (and pets!) could socialize and connect.

PROPOSING BENCH, TAMPA RIVERWALK

On Valentine's Day 2010, the city of Tampa unveiled its first-ever proposing bench, located along the Tampa Riverwalk halfway down the Curtis Hixon Waterfront Park lawn. "Every city has unique qualities, and certainly the fact that we have a beautiful waterfront that people enjoy on a daily basis is one of them," says Elizabeth Kurz, co-director for Friends of the Riverwalk, a nonprofit group that partners with the city to support the Riverwalk.[70] While she can't confirm if the proposing bench and nearby paver etched with the words "Will You Marry Me?" have inspired anyone yet, Kurz says the

Riverwalk has several customized pavers commemorating local engagements.

Proposing Bench, Curtis Hixon Park, Tampa, FL

MARCH MADNESS MARCHING BAND – LEXINGTON, KENTUCKY

Described as "a community punk rock marching band" by drummer, DJ and community advocate Mick Jeffries, March Madness is an all-volunteer marching band of more than 60 members that includes a flag team and, occasionally, fire dancers. The band began as an outgrowth of the buy local movement called First Lexington, but has taken on a life of its own. Today, March Madness performs all around the area and travels the country on its own dime to various events. Wherever the band goes, they proudly fly Lexington's flag.

When the band performs, March Madness provides a love note to the city of Lexington. Each performance is a rousing occasion that shows the band's enthusiasm and excitement, which reflects onto the city. You can't watch March Madness and not think about how much fun its players are having– and how wonderful it is that these people make an effort to do something magical for themselves, for their audience and for Lexington.

Clearly, people themselves can be love notes in some sense. Some people literally embody the love and affection they feel for cities; when you meet them, their passion and enthusiasm for their places is just palpable. Being with them makes you appreciate your city even more, and knowing that they are out there makes you happier and more fulfilled. In earlier chapters, I mentioned Bob Devin Jones from St. Petersburg's Studio@620 and Phil Cooley, a restaurant owner (and much more) from Detroit. Both men are exemplars of the idea that people can live their lives as love notes to their cities.

When we fall in love with a city, it is ultimately these love notes that we fall in love with. Too often they are deemed extra niceties rather than must-haves. But rather than regarding them as supplements to a city, we should be building narratives around these authentic and endearing elements. As I said before, no one ever fell in love with a city because its government fixed the potholes, but how many people have fallen in love with Chicago while standing under "The Bean" in Millennium Park, or with New Orleans while listening to jazz in Preservation Hall or while walking along Tampa's Riverwalk? Investing in things that make your city lovable as well as functional will pay back long-term dividends for your community.

Charles Landry, in his efforts to entice cities to think and act more creativity, likes to pose the provocative question of how much a hundred yards of asphalt typically costs. The answer is: tens of thousands of dollars, typically, and often much more for wide boulevards or highways. His point is that we should think about what we might be able to afford if we decided to make do with just a little less asphalt. Think of all the love that could be generated with a handful of love note projects if a community could figure out how to do with a quarter-mile less asphalt.

During the most recent economic crisis, we have seen city tax bases decimated and budgets slashed accordingly. Cities all over the world are trying to figure out how to do more with fewer resources. Clearly the crux of that effort consists in trying to maximize utility on limited resources so that the community sees the most benefit. But that outlook measures success only in terms of delivering the most basic attributes of functionality and safety. If communities also considered the possibility of increasing their constituents' happiness and love for the community, they might invest those resources differently. I am not suggesting we leave schools or fire departments wanting, but I am suggesting that if even a fraction of community resources were applied to making the city more lovable (say, the equivalent of a quarter mile or so of asphalt), such a shift would have an outsized impact on the city's narrative–the impression its residents and visitors have. A little love might make people forget about the cuts that reduced garbage pick up to once a week or the reduction of library hours on the weekend. In the current economic climate, service cuts are inevitable. The question then becomes do your residents love the city enough that those services cuts don't make them look to move to another place or psychically disengage from the city and fall down that continuum of engagement. In a personal relationship a little love goes a long way towards forgiving and overlooking someone's faults and missteps and it keeps people together when other forces might tear them apart. Love and affection for your city may let you overlook flaws and deficits that might otherwise lure you to other, often easier places to live.

This kind of love explains why cities like Detroit continue to fight on. Without that love, everyone who could would leave for easier cities with better amenities. Yet they don't and in fact, we sometimes see that the more challenging a place, the stronger the love and affection it engenders. This is something we will examine in more depth in the next chapter as we look at Detroit and New Orleans – two cities that generate outsized amounts of love from their citizens and are using those emotions as the fuel for their reinvention.

This love and affection is an asset that communities hold in their metaphoric bank. It accumulates over time through large and small acts and is lost with deficit and negative acts. And sometimes it is withdrawn and spent by cities when they need it to do something. When a city is able to raise its taxes or inconvenience its citizens with road work or development and they accept it, that is drawing on the dividend of community love. When people, of their own volition and at their own expense, do things for the community; from cleaning up a park to starting a street festival to creating a Facebook fan page – that is the benefit of love and emotional engagement. We will always do more for the people, the organizations and the cities we care about.

More Love Notes at www.fortheloveofcities.com.

Chapter Eight
For the Love of Cities

Cities are like parties. Some are loud; some are intimate; some are truly great; some suck. Some are just getting started, while some are winding down. Some parties are epic – think Mardi Gras in New Orleans or Rio during Carnival. But size alone does not make a great party. In fact, size can often scare off many would-be partygoers. But too small and you already know everyone there! Most parties, and cities, fall in between those polarities.

Building a great, creative city is akin to throwing a great party. The host– in this case the city– needs to provide a venue. It needs the basics: a variety of food, beverages and cocktails. It needs music that shifts throughout the night. It needs places to sit, places to stand, places to dance and– if you are lucky– places to hook up. It needs open areas where lots of people can congregate, and it needs intimate areas where you can have a one-on-one interaction with a new or old friend. Basically, the host of the party must anticipate the broad range of possible needs of a broad range of possible guests. The host needs to get the word out that the party is on and be present to make sure everyone is having a good time, that things are orderly (but

not too orderly!) and to clean up when something gets broken–
because something always gets broken.

Some parties have a theme – a construct that pervades the
entire party. Think of a costume party or a "black and white"
ball. The theme is the organizing principle, and the aspects
of the party flow from that theme. Themes can work for cities
when focus is required to bring together enough resources to
make change happen. Cities will adopt themes as a way of
making themselves attractive to residents and visitors and, thus
more economically viable. From the Bavarian themed city of
Leavenworth in Washington to the city of bookshops and book
festivals that is Hay-on-Wye in Wales, smaller places can create
distinct identity based on themes and even compete with much
larger places.

From those basics, it is up to the guests to create the party.
Most guests will be consumers of the party; they will eat, drink,
dance and have fun. But a few people will make the party great:
the piano playing friend who bangs out show tunes and pop
hits; the hipster DJ who spins the perfect mix; the hot bartender
who talks up the guests, keeps the drinks flowing and has a
smart retort for every pick up line; the brilliant artist who talks
passionately about his work; the comedian who is the life of
the party; the weird guy who brings his monkey; and the social
connector who knows everyone and glides from conversation to
conversation like an Olympic ice skater. These people make the
party, not because you paid or prompted them (OK, you paid the
bartender!) but because you created the space for them to operate,
doing what they instinctively do, which is to create something.

THE GREAT LOVERS

Most of this book has focused on how all of us can become
more emotionally engaged with our cities and the potential

benefits that such a change would hold for our communities. If we increase the love just a little bit across the board, our communities will be exponentially better for it. In these final sections, I want to focus on the few outliers at the far end of the continuum– the great "lovers" of cities. They, for the love of their cities, are responsible for an outsize contribution to making those cities into places and experiences that the rest of us enjoy. They are the ones who make the party into something special. They are the co-creators of communities.

WHO ARE THE CO-CREATORS?

Who are these great lovers of cities? On the continuum of engagement, they are the outliers, the extreme group at the far right of the spectrum. They are the ones who are truly "in love" with their community. They start things. They make things happen. They inspire others to get in the game. They educate people. They connect people. They are tastemakers and trendsetters. They are the 1% who built Wikipedia.

Co-creators are starters. Starters are the first ones in the pool, the first ones on the dance floor and the catalysts that literally make things happen. Claire Nelson is the co-founder of Open City, a forum for aspiring and existing small business owners in Detroit, and a drafter of the Detroit Declaration. She launched one of the first new retail businesses in her Midtown neighborhood when she opened the Bureau of Urban Living, a small design store similar to a Crate & Barrel, in the Canfield Lofts Building. Not only did she start her own business– she actively recruited friends and colleagues to start other businesses in the area as well. When a space became vacant next to her shop, she explains, "I begged everyone I knew to open something there." Her efforts paid off. A design company called Two Birds opened next door, and Claire has called it "my greatest achievement so far" because she gained a neighbor and someone who shares the same love of place.

Claire Nelson at her shop The Bureau of
Urban Living, photo by Vanessa Miller

Co-creators are builders– sometimes literally builders. From Phil Cooley in Michigan (who personally renovated the building where his restaurant now sits) to Phil Holoubek (the Lexington developer who insists on density, great design and public art in his projects), builders are shaping the built environment and making it more than just functional and safe. They are building community.

Co-creators are educators– like the Emerging Cleveland project, which shows people their city through new eyes.

Co-creators are entrepreneurs, such as the Vines brothers from STL Style. Randy and Jeff Vines started the company because they wanted to market their pride in St. Louis– and they discovered a significant audience. "It was never our goal to get rich peddling t-shirts at all. It was really about just our passion for the city," said Jeff Vines.

Co-creators are connectors. They are the people that can dial you into a community because they know everybody. Grace Wilson in New Orleans is such a connector. First with the Lieutenant Governor's office, then the Convention and Visitors Bureau and now with the New Orleans Museum of Art, Grace connects people and ideas. She helped me meet and interview most of the New Orleans-related people who appear in this book (thanks again Grace!). She connects with so many people, but she doesn't do it in a glad-handing, sales person kind of way. She does it, and does it well, because she loves the city and wants to see it and its people thrive.

Sean Mann is the man behind the "Let's Save Michigan" campaign, which is part of his day job with the Michigan Municipal League. But even in his spare time he is a connector of people in Detroit. In 2010 he started the Detroit City Futbol League, which created teams from eleven of Detroit's historic neighborhoods. To play on a team, you had to live in that neighborhood. And each team was affiliated with a local bar that hosted the rotating happy hour that followed each game. In its first year, over 400 people signed up, and several people told Sean that they actually moved into the city so they could play.

Some co-creators are bridge builders, a special kind of connector who brings people across divides of race, class, politics and religion. They often do this at personal risk, but they are able to do so because they have earned respect from both sides of the conflict. Trevor Douglas runs a community center in Lurgan, a small town southwest of Belfast in Northern Ireland. Lurgan has the unfortunate history of being part of the "Murder Triangle" during The Troubles and today remains a flashpoint for sectarian violence. Douglas is part of the Protestant Church there, but he has been able to connect with the Catholic community as well. And in doing this, he has had to deal with the paramilitary groups on both sides.

"I have a love for this town and for its people. I don't always love its politics, but I love its people. And I love the community that was here. And that has been destroyed over the last 30 years, but there was a great family feeling around Lurgan, and it would be my hope to see that brought back into this community again, regardless of religious makeup or denomination," said Douglas. To do that he said, "You have to get close to people. You have to have relationships with people. You have to have respect for each other. And when you get to that point, anything can be accomplished."

Co-creators are provocateurs. Recall Justin Langlois and Broken City Lab from Chapter 6. They started out as a guerilla performance/protest art movement in Windsor. They were eventually embraced by the city, which now works with them as a partner, but they originated as provocateurs. Wanting change to happen can be seen as rebellion, particularly by those most entrenched by the status quo.

Co-creators are more likely than not to be tastemakers; they drive the opinions and set the zeitgeist in their respective communities. While some may actually be in positions where they write, or blog or overtly create opinions, many others simply shape opinions by what they do— what restaurants they go to, what bars they drink in, what openings they go to, what coffee shops they hold their meetings in. All of these things are noted by the consuming class.

Cherylyn Tompkins is a co-creator, and her job is to find and expose all that is fabulous about New Orleans. Known as "Miss FabuNOLA," she blogs and posts to thousands of people in the Crescent City. What she says is cool and fabulous becomes cool and fabulous. Julia Gorzka founded Brand Tampa in 2008, and her site has become a hub for what is cool and interesting in region. Ning, the social media platform used by Brand Tampa, has highlighted her as a best practice in using their system. To several thousand followers on social media, Julia is the definitive "Tampa girl." Neither Julia or Cherylyn thought about making money from their initial efforts. They both love their communities and wanted to use their time and talents to make something happen. In doing that, they have become tastemakers and trend-setters for their cities.

Co-creators are champions. They are St. Petersburg's Bob Devin Jones & Detroit's Phil Cooley. They are the co-creators that the other co-creators look up to and take their cues from. They are the champion's champions. Every community has one, sometimes more than one. Find them, ask them what you can do to help and give them room to do what they naturally do!

A QUICK NOTE ABOUT PRESTIGE & SOCIAL STATUS – ROLE OF EGO

As psychologist Nancy Etcoff points out, "we are acutely aware of our social status and always seek to further & increase it."[71] To deny that ego and status plays a part in the process for the co-creators is clearly erroneous. Rather, I suspect that ego is a necessary component to the co-creator. Every co-creator I interviewed or have ever encountered had confidence and some ego about their work in the sense that all of them saw what they were doing as important. And a little ego is important just as having some sense of self importance and self worth is a necessary component to being able to put yourself and your work out there for the world to see.

The intrinsic motivation of co-creators is hard to define and certainly will vary with each individual. The Italians have a word—*fiero*—for which there is no direct English translation; roughly, it means taking pride in accomplishing a task, particularly a difficult task. I believe that co-creators take a special satisfaction in what they do because it is hard and, whether they acknowledge it or not, they know that most people cannot do what they do.

What I have found many co-creators have in common is that their ego is not diminished or challenged by other co-creators. In fact, co-creators celebrate the efforts of others and do not see them as competition but rather colleagues and sources of inspiration. In a sense, they perform for these other co-creators knowing that their peers, better than most, understand and fully appreciate what it takes to make things happen. It's like playing music. To lay people, the music we see on stage is cool and fun, and we enjoy it. Great musicians make it look effortless to us. But other musicians see the complexity and the virtuosity on stage because they play too.

WHY CO-CREATORS MATTER

The co-creative community is the sustaining lifeblood of a party and of a community, yet we don't think about them as a distinct group with common characteristics and interests. We all know someone who is a co-creator, and we recognize what a blow to the community it would be to lose them– or worse, to have them lose interest in the community and stop doing what they intrinsically do.

Co-creators produce the interesting, the memorable, the unique, the fun and the lovable aspects of our community. They aren't responsible for every last thing, of course, but they do "punch above their weight" when it comes to creating lovable experiences. Co-creators make the content that most of us consume. When Chris Miller headed up the Creative Coast Initiative in Savannah, GA, he described his approach to recruiting talent to the area as focusing on "content creators" and not on "content consumers." "If you got the creators, you will of course have consumers," he noted.

Some co-creators will work with the deliberate goal of making a difference in their community. They influence others just as a natural byproduct of their desire to create and make things happen. That desire is the most common attribute of co-creators–not some benevolent notion of community good. They want to make things happen, and if the community benefits from those efforts – cool.

But whether or not they intend to be, co-creators are the centers of community energy that the rest of us orbit; they are the glue that connects us to so many other people. When we lose one of these centers, the gravitational shift can throw many people out of balance.

Sometimes circumstances have chased off most of the other people who typically create communities. When things get tough in a city, many will opt for greener pastures– even folks who have strong emotional connections to their place. Sometimes you are left with just the folks who truly love a place, and that is not necessarily all bad. Sometimes those co-creators are the only thing standing between death and despair in communities.

TWO TOUGH CITIES

In my travels around the world, I have met many people who are passionately "in love" with their cities. These people champion and defend their places better than any Chamber of Commerce ever could. And I have learned that every place, no matter how bad or decayed it may seem, has someone who loves it. Yet two cities stand out in my mind, in part because of their extraordinary circumstances, of course, but also due to the depth and volume of the passion and devotion that their champions have for them. They are also places that have generated a prodigious number of co-creators: Detroit and New Orleans.

Prior to Hurricane Katrina, both New Orleans and Detroit fit the description of the old, decaying post-industrial city that was in decline due to shifts in industry and the economy. Both were dying the death of a thousand cuts, losing industry, jobs, talent and purpose as well.

Following Katrina and the financial meltdown of 2008-2009, we see that both cities are victims of human failures. New Orleans was the victim of a cataclysmic event that happened in a day but had been lying in wait for decades in the form of poor and under-engineered levee systems; Detroit was the victim of a cataclysmic economic shift that happened over decades, as its leaders refused to change with the world, and came to point in the fall of 2008. Both are among the world's most challenged cities, yet both have engendered tremendous love. And I believe it will be that love that brings them back and reinvents them for the 21st century.

DETROIT

In 2007 and 2008 I spent a lot of time in Detroit when I produced the second Creative Cities Summit there. I got to know the city, and what I found there was vastly different from what the media had been telling me about Detroit. The media narrative depicted Detroit as a post-industrial ruin scarred by job loss, failing industry and crime. All of these phenomena exist in Detroit, but the media never showed me the pockets of dynamic activity, urban regeneration and entrepreneurship that are happening there. And the media did not prepare me for the overwhelming number of people who passionately love "The D." I was– and am still– amazed at the numbers and the intensity of the champions of that city. It seems as if they have taken the attitude that the world is against them and rallied behind that idea to make Detroit their cause. If Detroit is to rise again, it will be because of this group of co-creators who refuse to give up on the city.

Tyree Guyton is the world-renowned artist who started the Heidelberg Project in 1986 in the tough McDougall-Hunt neighborhood of East Detroit. Turning abandoned houses into works of art using found objects and dazzling colors, Guyton is in many ways the grandfather of the grassroots, creative approach to city building. Jenneane Whitfield is the Executive Director of the Heidelberg Project and Guyton's wife. She noted that Detroit is "a city of cultural originators" whose creativity had long been overshadowed by the dominance of the auto industry. Today, with that industry in transition, she believes the city can create a "positive epidemic of arts and culture that will be Detroit's new industry."

Race plays a subtle but evident role in the conversation. While many young, white entrepreneurs such as Nelson and Cooley garner media attention, pioneers such as Guyton are somewhat discounted. Whitfield notes, "there is a culture here that overlooks the efforts of people who live here." In a city that is 83% African-American, that translates into racial terms.

Larry Mongo is a long-standing African-American business owner in Detroit. With regards to the young, mostly white kids coming back into the city, he offers a particularly cogent perspective. "A lot of my buddies, they started saying, 'Ah, man, these white kids are takin' over the city.' I say, 'Naw, they're filling the gaps. They left first, we filled in gaps. We left, (now) they're filling in the gaps.'"[72]

Fortunately, the young leaders I spoke with– including Nelson and Cooley– were highly respectful of Guyton and other local leaders. "Other people ascribe the whole 'you're saving the city' stuff but I resist that," Nelson said. "Living here eight years now you have to respect the things that were already here. I am not a pioneer, I am following people who have done this for decades."

Eric Cedo directs the Lifton Institute for Media Skills, a film and media trade school set up in Michigan to train unemployed auto work factory folks in skilled trades for the film and television industry. In the spring of 2010, the institute graduated its first class of 100 retrained workers, ready to fill positions created by Michigan's aggressive tax credits for the film and television industry. Prior to his work with the Lifton Institute, Cedo was the head of CreateDetroit, a grassroots (first generation) creative economy initiative aimed at attracting and retaining talent. He is a passionate and provocative voice when it comes to Detroit, and he pulls no punches when speaks of his city.

"This region, this city is not a place to come and be at ease," he said. "It's not a place to come and just be one of many, to blend in. You almost lose your anonymity in Detroit, because it's just so sparse in terms of talent and people. So the people that are here, the people that do choose to stay, can make an immediate impact."

"You don't go to Chicago to make a difference in Chicago. You don't go to New York feeling like, 'I am going to leave my imprint on New York.' I am not going to New York to make New York. I am going to New York to make me. In Detroit, you feel differently. I go to Detroit because I want to have an imprint on Detroit. I want to build. I want to create. I want to make something of the city. Not just make something of my life, but I want what I make of my life to be a part of something bigger than myself" said Cedo.

Phil Cooley concurs. "If I move to New York, I have no say in what happens in that city. And that's a ship you can't steer. If I'm here and I give a damn, and I actually go out and I'm part of the community, I can actually do something and make a difference in Detroit."[73]

Not surprisingly, these change agents in Detroit all know each other and are fans of each other's work. Cedo points to Cooley: "Phil has the opportunity constantly to expand and build, and he just doesn't want to. He's doing what he's doing because he feels like he is doing it for a reason, for a purpose. It's more than a restaurant. It's community building. It's neighborhood building."

Cooley exemplifies the new spirit of camaraderie among this new generation – when another guy wanted to open a restaurant down the street from his, Cooley not only helped him pull permits, he actually built tabletops for the other restaurant owner at no charge.[74]

The New York Times took note of Cooley and said:

Maybe it's that adage that nothing brings a community closer than having a common enemy. For the restaurateurs, the residents, the urban farmers and the community activists now working to reshape the city, the enemy is Detroit's own reputation. They know they will succeed only if they are a part of a larger, collective success, one that makes downtown a thriving destination again, and so they're working together to make it happen.[75]

Collective success has required collective support and some wildly creative ways to pool resources in an otherwise resource-starved town.

Soup is a monthly gathering of co-creators and Detroit supporters. Founded in early 2010 by artist Kate Daughdrill and musician Jessica Hernandez, the group meets monthly at a restaurant, the Mexican Town Bakery, for dinner and presentations of project ideas from the audience. Everyone pays $5 to participate, and at the end of the evening, a vote decides which project will receive the money collected at the door. In the past seven months, proposals including a photography project about the Rustbelt and a coloring book drawn by a local artist have been funded. Soup has grown steadily over the months with the August 2010 meeting being the largest to date with 120 attendees.

Kate Daughdrill, Detroit's Soup, photo by Vanessa Miller

Jerry Paffendorf, a recent émigré from Brooklyn, created the brilliant Loveland Project (www.makeloveland.com). Paffendorf purchased 3000 square feet of property in Detroit for $500. Since then he has started selling off that property one square inch at a time to people who want to make an investment in the city of Detroit. "The inches become like little shares in the city," Paffendorf said. "Even such a lightweight form of ownership has a really cool psychological effect. Even if they bought the inches on a whim, it would bring people into the city a little bit more."[76]

The "inchvestors" are provided deeds and plots on a grid of Loveland online. There, inchvestors can see who is in their "neighborhood" and connect with other Detroit supporters. The money raised by selling these inches is then used to fund other projects around the city including Imagination Station, a clean-up project that seeks to turn two blighted buildings in the shadow of Central Train Station into public art space. (Interestingly, one of Paffendorf's partners in the project is Phil Cooley, whose restaurant is just a block away from the site.)

There is a growing sense of momentum in Detroit amongst this small DIY-city crowd. "There's an excitement here," said Dale Dougherty, editor and publisher of Make magazine, which spawned the Maker Faire, an event celebrating arts, crafts, science and the do it yourself spirit. "There's a sense that it's a frontier again, that it's open, that you can do things without a lot of people telling you, 'No, you can't do that.'"[77] Maker Faire had its Detroit debut at the end of July 2010, and it drew over 22,000 people for demonstrations that included wind- powered cars and fire-spewing bicycles at the Henry Ford Museum.

NEW ORLEANS

New Orleans today may be the most exciting city in America because all of it– from infrastructure, to institutions, to leadership– is being rebuilt. There is a sense of purpose, possibility and opportunity in New Orleans that is palpable. From movie stars to students, talent is flowing to the region in waves. The young professional group, 504ward, which formed post-Katrina to network these newcomers into the fabric of the community, describes the talent bonanza: "For decades, the New Orleans area has suffered from a 'brain drain' as recent college graduates left New Orleans in pursuit of opportunities elsewhere. A silver lining to Hurricane Katrina has been the influx of college educated, mission-driven 'brain gainers.'"[78]

Today New Orleans is attracting talent, particularly young talent, in record numbers. The City estimated that by the summer of 2008, more than 3,000 new college educated young people had arrived in New Orleans.[79] Lauren Thom, the founder of Fleurty Girl, was living in Baton Rouge and working as a news reporter after Katrina. But she could not stay away from her hometown. As she eloquently told me "New Orleans called her people and brought me home." Both those who have returned to the city like Thom and newcomers are there because they want to be there, they have a passion for the city and they want to be part of the rebuilding process.

This includes movie stars. In the Lower 9th Ward, more than 4,000 homes were destroyed. In 2007 Brad Pitt toured the area and, in that spirit of making things happen, established the Make It Right Foundation with the goal to build 150 green, affordable and well-designed homes in the devastated neighborhood. Since then, the organization has raised millions of dollars, received the support of world class architects and builders from all over the world and, as of the summer of 2010, was well along the way to delivering the 150 homes it pledged to complete. According to the US Green Building Council, the Lower 9th Ward is now the "largest, greenest neighborhood of single family homes in America,"[80] as all of the Make It Right homes have been certified LEED Platinum for energy efficiency and sustainability.

LEED certified Make It Right house in Lower 9th Ward

The class of newcomers has quickly distinguished themselves too. Robert Fogarty is a 27-year-old social entrepreneur, originally from Omaha, Nebraska. He came to New Orleans in 2007 as part of the national service program AmeriCorps. (Interestingly he told me that, prior to devoting himself to New Orleans, he had been in New York City fresh out of college and working a traditional job as a recruiter for the finance industry.) In New Orleans, he served in the Mayor's Office as Volunteer Coordinator for two years until March 2009.

That summer he formed the not-for-profit Evacuteer to train people to assist in the evacuation of citizens most in need of help during a crisis. And he set out to secure funding for the new organization.

He tells the story on the organization's website:

"I began the traditional ways of raising capital to fund evacuteer. org as the volunteer executive director and chairman of the board. I submitted our first grant application, a request for $25,000, to one of the well-respected private foundations in the City.

367 other organizations did too.

The day I received a polite rejection email beginning "We very much appreciate the thought and effort you dedicated..." I knew that relying only on private and foundational support—especially in the economic climate of 2009—was neither feasible nor in line with the social entrepreneurial spirit that has become a highlight of New Orleans' recovery."

Inspired by a friend, Fogarty set up a fund raising photo station at the 2009 Bye Bye Hurricane Party and invited people to write "love notes" to the city on their hands with markers. He posted the photos online, and immediately people went mad for them. The photos were reposted, blogged, Tweeted and shared on Facebook. Fogarty had tapped into something simple but very profound - the love and affection that people have for their city.

So he started a photography business called Dear New Orleans just to continue creating such love notes. In February 2010, on the same day the Saints won the Super Bowl, the business held its first "Dear New Orleans" session at a local bar called the Rendon Inn. Over a hundred portraits were taken that day and a new business was launched.

Dear New Orleans is a love note to the city. The photos the company makes (with the participation of Nola residents and visitors) are powerful, fun and wonderful declarations of people's love for the city. And they become an incredible tool for spreading and increasing love for the city! As people post and share their photos with their social networks, they are reminding other people of the relationship they have with their city and (hopefully) making them appreciate that connection to New Orleans. The best part is that Dear Orleans has been so successful that it funds the not for profit Evacuteer. And Dear New Orleans has expanded to Baltimore (with other cities pending), and Fogarty is working on "Dear World" for a 2011 launch.)

When I interviewed him, Fogarty was reluctant to attach too much import to himself, though he clearly believes in the power of Dear New Orleans. He told me that while he blogged during his stint in AmeriCorps, one native resident cautioned him about being one of those outsiders coming to New Orleans to save it from itself. It's a lesson he clearly carries with him today. Fogarty calls himself more of "role player," saying that, like most of the newcomers to New Orleans, "we are lagniappe here." Lagniappe (pronounced LAN-yap) is that something extra given to the customer such as the baker's dozen 13th donut. The newcomers are that something extra that has been added to New Orleans. Fogarty worries that guys like him get too much attention for being newcomers and says the focus should be on those natives who are doing amazing things.

Robert Fogarty of Dear New Orleans and Evacuteer,
photo courtesy Dear New Orleans

Fogarty is part of the wave of young, socially minded, community building entrepreneurs at the heart of the rebuilding of New Orleans. He describes that special breed of entrepreneur: "We're in a club and the password is that pit-of-your stomach feeling. That draw-it-up idea and see-it-actually-working feeling. That undeniable longing of wanting to do better today than you did yesterday."[81]

That "club" of entrepreneurs can be found in several new workspaces that have emerged to house this influx of business. Four entrepreneurial hubs have arisen in the past few years since the hurricane: Entrepreneur's Row, the Icehouse, the I.P. (short for Intellectual Property) and the Entergy Innovation Center. These are not incubators but rather places that bring together both established businesses and start-ups. Tim Williamson, founder of Idea Village, a not for profit support organization for entrepreneurs, says: "New Orleans is becoming this national laboratory of the next generation of entrepreneurial leaders,"[82] and these facilities allow for a "clustering of like-minded entrepreneurs to build their businesses together."[83] In 2009, Idea Village and Greater New Orleans, Inc., the regional economic development agency, refurbished the 85,000-square-foot building that is now the I.P..

Williamson, a native of Louisiana who, like many, left the state early in his career only to find his way back, says "if you look at the people who have come since Katrina, there has been this influx of talent that has come to New Orleans initially to help, but now they are here to stay and live and to grow new companies. ... This is a once in a lifetime opportunity to reinvent an American city."[84]

Entrepreneurs' Row is the brainchild of developer Sean Cummings. Founded in 2008 along with Start Up New Orleans, the organization recruits companies and entrepreneurs to the city. Cummings has personally found and recruited companies to New Orleans, even providing free rent to some. Today Entrepreneurs' Row houses nine companies. The bar in Cummings' hotel Loa, has become the entrepreneurs' hang out–the place where deals are done and connections made. "We must... recruit entrepreneurs who are drawn to a joyful quality of life... Entrepreneurs are reinventing New Orleans, like Prague after the curtain, like Milan, like a smaller Seattle[85] – [New Orleans is also] a great waterfront city with a terrific music scene and great artisan community,"[86] said Cummings.

"We're seeing the exact same thing here that we saw in the Bay Area in the mid '90s," said Michael Hecht, president of Greater New Orleans, Inc., a nonprofit economic development agency. He moved to New Orleans in early 2006 after living in both San Francisco and New York. "There's a sense of opportunity and possibility [here], combined with people who have the horsepower to actualize those possibilities."[87]

Artists, too, are catching the social entrepreneurship wave and using their craft to rebuild the city. Kirsha Kaechele is an artist/architect who arrived in New Orleans in 2000. After Katrina, she returned to the city and started KK Projects in six abandoned houses, inviting artists from all over the world to use the houses as their canvases. That the houses are located in a neighborhood "where the residents don't typically get to go to MOMA," said Kaechele, is part of the project's appeal for her. She has also orchestrated a series of "feasts" in these same neighborhoods that bring tables out into the streets and invites local residents to dine with artists and visitors from all over the world in mash-ups of food, art, community and bridge-building, creating "unlikely connections between different societal groups." Kaechele's latest project involved living and making art communally with other artists for 30 days in a renovated structure that was actually part of the original Eiffel Tower. I interviewed her on the day she was scheduled to go into the structure for 30 days. We toured the space, and it was far more of a construction site than a readymade space for art! But Kirsha said, "I have been in love with this building for years," and she was looking forward to the process.

Part of the reason that artists and entrepreneurs find New Orleans so appealing is its openness. "No one tells you that you can't do something, and you don't need to stand in line... going through a bunch of bureaucratic sludge," said Kaechele.

When I asked her about her relationship with the city she laughed and called it a sometimes-abusive relationship. "I really love it, but it is hard... and sometimes I fantasize about checking out and going to a functional place," said Kaechele.

But functional can be overrated according to Jeremy Cooker, a tech entrepreneur in New Orleans. He and his wife relocated to Tampa immediately following Katrina. He noted one day that there was a water leak outside his house in the suburbs of Tampa. He called the city and to his amazement, the next day a work crew came out to fix the leaking sprinkler head. "So this is what a functional city looks like" he thought. "That did not and would not happen in New Orleans." Despite Tampa being a "functional" city, he and his wife returned to New Orleans in 2007.

August 2010 marked the five-year anniversary of Hurricane Katrina. The media returned en masse to New Orleans. Most of the coverage was positive and highlighted the growing entrepreneurial spirit that has arisen. While a tremendous amount of work is yet to be done, New Orleans has managed to turn a crisis into an opportunity and has used it to invigorate and inspire their community and the rest of the nation as well.

HOW DETROIT IS DIFFERENT FROM NEW ORLEANS

The disaster that was Katrina is very different from the death by a thousand cuts that Detroit has suffered. Consequently the Michigan city has not responded in the same dramatic fashion as New Orleans– which poses the question, do you need a complete disaster to shake loose the ossified sediment in communities that prevents change?

Unlike Detroit, New Orleans was able to sweep away the old ways of doing business by clearing out the corridors of power and opening up opportunity. Tim Williamson of Idea Village said, "what Katrina did was fracture the old networks and help create new ones. What was missing in New Orleans was more people like us."[88]

Today, residents of New Orleans have been able to translate that gap into the promise of jobs for those who come there. What is striking is the popular notion that there are no jobs in Detroit and in Michigan. That is not exactly true. There are no manufacturing jobs in Michigan, but there are hundreds of open positions in the knowledge and creative economy that go unfilled. The narrative generated about Detroit focuses on the loss of jobs and despite the half-truth of it, that story is what people have come to believe. In contrast, the narrative now around New Orleans is highly inspiring, even considering the negative aspects of the city– and that is a significant contrast with Detroit.

If you go talk to residents of New Orleans, there is a sense that they are on a mission. And that perception is reflected in public awareness. The small group of co-creators I have met in Detroit are also on a mission, but that mission has yet to be broadly understood across the city.

Dan Gilmartin, Executive Director of the Michigan Municipal League said to me, "Many of our leaders are trying to recreate the economy we had here in the 1950's and 1960's. They still believe that is possible. And until we break from that thinking, we cannot move fully forward." Gilmartin is representative of many up and coming leaders in the region who are battling with decades of tradition and industrial era thinking.

Claire Nelson, the local shop owner from Detroit, thinks the problem runs even deeper. "Amongst our leaders there is not an optimism about the future of Detroit, and there is even a mild contempt for the city with a lot of higher ups. People like us down on the ground don't see that. If you are at the top of the Renaissance Towers looking down on the city... you're just not feeling it the same way as those of us at the street level...

Most development decisions seem to reflect that they don't feel it and don't truly believe. "

When I asked Richard Florida about this challenge for traditional leadership, he noted that this was the critical issue for Detroit and other cities. The "corporate and political class" of the city has to understand the role of this bottom-up energy and not squelch that enthusiasm. And he is not sure they really understand what to do with this movement.

Recently, Crain's Detroit Business magazine challenged their local ad agencies and freelance designers to come up with a compelling message that would help retain under-30 talent. The challenge was taken up across the region, and in June 2010 the winning campaign was announced. Created by a team at Detroit's famed design school, the College for Creative Studies, the winning entry focused on Detroit's affordability. It featured a beautiful young woman in a bar with the tagline: "A ten is just as hard to approach in Detroit as she is in Chicago. *Except in Detroit, you can actually afford to buy her a drink."

When asked about the thinking behind the ad, the winning team declared that they had discovered that affordability was a key reason many recent grads stayed in market. The ad got a full page run in the July 26, 2010, issue of Advertising Age.

Clever, yes, and reasonable, certainly, but I think an ad like this totally misses the real opportunity in Detroit, which is that ability to make a difference in the community. Interestingly, other finalists produced campaigns to convince young professionals that blight was opportunity, danger was excitement, and that leaving Detroit was abandoning adventure. One tagline: "Moving is just running with a U-Haul. Your City is calling." That message is gutsy, and while it may not appeal to the broad mass of young professionals, it certainly hits home with the mission driven. Another showed a montage of young faces with the headline "Detroit – Where 25 is the new 40," which recognizes that young people are doing things in Detroit that they would be hard pressed to accomplish at a young age in other places.

Marketing 101 teaches us that using words and images like "blight," "danger" and "abandonment" is not traditionally done.   But Detroit needs something far more than a good marketing campaign.   It needs to be able to say what New Orleans doesn't have to actually say because it is obvious; it needs to be able to say "we are a fucked up ruin of a post-industrial city that has made many mistakes and is hanging on by guts and determination.   But we are hanging on here and looking for people who want to come to a place that is wide open for possibilities.   It is hard here, but hard makes it great, hard makes it interesting and hard makes it meaningful.   Other places would be lucky to have your talents but we <u>need</u> you.   Want to come to a city that is grateful and welcoming of your talent, one that <u>you</u> can help to rebuild and make a difference?   Then Detroit is the city for you."   But will they have the self-awareness and courage to do so?

"We used to have a saying when I was running CreateDetroit," said Eric Cedo.   "You can go to another city where it's paint by numbers, or you can come to Detroit where it's a blank canvas.   Builders welcome; dwellers need not apply."

Hallie Bram of Cleveland sees her city in same light: "There are creators, and there are dwellers.   If you're a dweller, you go to Chicago.   You go to New York, Boston, or Los Angeles.   If you're a creator, you go to Cleveland.   You go because you can create, you can write the future, and the community wants it and will support you."

"Real entrepreneurs," said Richard Florida, "those who want to build something new,   sometimes pick "frontier locations," places where they can mold the environment to help them reach their desired goals, like the tech pioneers of Silicon Valley in the late 60s and 70s, or Hollywood's early moguls."[89]

Walter Isaacson, CEO of the Aspen Institute and native New Orleanian, told participants of the 2010 New Orleans Entrepreneurship Week (event created by Idea Village), that the founders of America were true entrepreneurs, and that the "new founding fathers and mothers of the United States are the people of New Orleans."[90]

Could this approach work?   Ask New Orleans if they have had to work to attract young talent in the last couple of years. Talent is flocking there because of opportunity, a sense of purpose and the ability to make a difference.

NEW FRONTIERS

In his 2008 book, *Why New Orleans Matters*, Tom Piazza captures the essence of what the city has become:

New Orleans has, in fact, become a kind of frontier town, with all the opportunities (for good and bad), the unpredictability (good and bad), the violence, and the sense that one's own actions might conceivably have an effect on one's environment. Like any frontier, it attracts adventurers, profiteers, romantics, desperadoes, and those who want to remake themselves in some way, to rewrite the map of possibility. It also has been attracting a startling number of idealistic and tough people from around the country, mostly young but not exclusively so, who see a chance to make a difference. Unlike most frontier towns, this one also has a long, rich and ongoing history.

Matt Wisdom, CEO of Turbo Squid, a 3D digital media company in New Orleans, describes why his business stayed put in the aftermath of Katrina: "It felt like the Wild West.

And it made us feel like we were pioneers rebuilding something from the ground up."[91]

For the small but growing DIY city making community in Detroit, they already know it is a frontier even if the majority of residents don't understand that. "We are in neighborhoods that are alive... if you embed yourself in that world, you can't help but fall in love with the city. But if you live out in the suburbs and drive into the city to work in your tower, you're just not gonna feel the love," said Claire Nelson.

Other cities are tapping into this idea as well. In Cleveland, I spoke with Hallie Bram and her partner Eric Kogelschatz, who moved to Cleveland from Boston, and they noted, "if you're creative, if you're passionate, and if you want to make change, I can't think of a better place to be. In many ways, it's like the Wild West. If you want to do something positive, big or small, it's possible here." To that end they became the local producers of TEDx Cleveland, which debuted in the city in 2010.

Braddock Pennsylvania is a small town outside of Pittsburgh and an unlikely frontier for a creative renaissance. A satellite of Pittsburgh that grew with the steel industry, Braddock has suffered a loss of purpose and people with the decline of the steel industry in Western Pennsylvania. From its heyday in the 1950s, Braddock has lost 90% of its population, coming in today at just under 3,000 people. But the city's charismatic Mayor John Fetterman refuses to let the city die. Fetterman certainly does not look like a typical politician. With a shaved head, goatee and an imposing six and half feet tall and over 300 pounds, he might be a villain out of a James Bond film. But the Harvard educated Mayor has almost single handedly put Braddock back on the map with his unusual efforts to rebuild the city. He bought the warehouse he now lives in for $2000 and renovated it into loft space. He "married his city" with a tattoo of the number "15104" after he was elected in 2005 by a single vote.

"15104 is Braddock's zip code, and I got that tattooed on my forearm immediately after the election as way to remind myself and to let others know I'm in this for the long haul"[92] says Fetterman. He also bears a more grim reminder of the city on his other forearm, where he has tattooed the dates of murders in the city during his tenure. So far there are five dates on his right arm.

From purchasing buildings to lobbying for a carbon cap to creating a section on the city's website called "Ruins" (a photo gallery of the ruins of Braddock), Fetterman's actions don't say politics as usual.

One of his novel approaches involves a partnership with the Levi Straus company. In conjunction with Levi's, Braddock is featured in a series of short films that document the "frontier" aspects of the city. In one piece, the film shows a series of Braddock residents starting their day and going to work in this decaying city. A child's voice is heard saying "Perhaps the world breaks on purpose so that we will have work to do" as images show people at work rebuilding parts of Braddock, including the installation of a beautiful stained glass window in their rebuilt community center. "People think there aren't frontiers anymore. They can't see how frontiers are all around us" intones the film as the camera tracks headlong down a street in Braddock.[93] (see video here: http://bit.ly/braddockvideo)

Not everyone can thrive in a frontier town. Grace Wilson was a 24-year PR professional in New Orleans when Katrina struck. She recalled that in the months that followed she understood why so many people left. "If I had family and kids, if I needed a functioning school system and a functioning hospital system I would have left." Being 20-something and able to "couch surf" for months allowed Grace to stay in the city she loves. "I was in a position where I could pour everything I had into the city. I could be selfish that way. But so many other people around me, they had to get out, and I understand that."

Crime and violence are also an issue. "It's an extreme city," noted architect/designer Jeff Sturges of Detroit[94], who bears a facial scar from an armed robbery attempt. Sturges, a New York City transplant who works with the FabLab and HackerSpace in Detroit remains undaunted. In Detroit, scars are almost a badge of honor for some. "I don't know a single person that has lived in Detroit for any significant amount of time, let's say more than three or four years, that hasn't been robbed, or their car broken into, or something like that. Yeah, you get robbed in Detroit," said Eric Cedo.

New Orleans has embraced the frontier mentality– it has had to. It now attracts co-creators and other talent in record numbers. Detroit hangs on in part because of the core group of co-creators it retains, while the broader community still clings to past notions of the city's economy, status and grandeur. Some would point out that Detroit is neither a frontier nor a blank canvas because of the many people who never left, and they would be correct. I speak instead of the idea of the frontier– an attitude, if not an actual open vista. Many people find the idea of the frontier a hard one to accept, but I believe it is in becoming the next frontier that Detroit could find the people and energy it needs to remake itself. If it works in New Orleans, it can work in Detroit.

BEING & BECOMING

German historian and philosopher Oswald Spengler, in his book *The Decline of the West* (1918), classified civilizations as either in a state of "becoming" or of "being." In the becoming stage, creativity, innovation, culture and the other dynamic elements of the society were active. Once the civilization achieved "being," once it metaphorically "arrived," it began a long process of decline and decay. The developed Western world has broadly achieved "being." But there are a few places in that world, some because of planning and some because of happenstance, that have been pushed back to the point of "becoming" yet again. They are frontiers but with the advantage of history, building on rich legacies and stories. And that state of building (or rebuilding) is exciting. It can draw entrepreneurs and adventurers and energize them with a true sense of purpose.

The American spirit is tied to the idea of the frontier. Our great legends of expansion (including our historic move westward) are predicated on the idea of the next frontier, where hope and opportunity awaits. This optimism and idealization of the frontier is part of American identity. We seek out opportunity like plants track the moving sun; it is something we must do. What we have found in the comfort of the 20th century, characterized by American prosperity, is that we lost our frontiers. Success, comfort and being the only superpower made us the privileged children of wealthy parents. We lost our frontiers in that long line of American success. What cities like New Orleans, Detroit, Cleveland and Braddock show us is that we are good with frontiers, we may even be at our best when we are making things, free from too many restraints and rules, seeking opportunities, making money, making meaning and making a difference.

THE LURE OF THE FRONTIER

Why do the most entrepreneurial and creative people in Detroit stay when so many others flee the city for Chicago or

Indianapolis? Why do young professionals head to New Orleans when the levee system has yet to be modernized and many basic institutions such as the school system and health care remain significantly under staffed and under resourced? Why do these places attract so many passionate co-creators when other places, arguably with more opportunity and certainly an easier lifestyle, go wanting? What do the people who move to these cities see in them? What are they chasing that motivates them to go where so many others literally fear to tread?

Meaning. The same thing that Hallie Bram and Phil Cooley talked about: making a difference and making things happen. For a growing number of people, the opportunity to make meaningful contributions, to create something, to see their efforts manifest in tangible results is a potent aphrodisiac. From Boomers through Gen X to the Millennials, these groups have enjoyed a standard of living that is the envy of the world. With that comfort has come an underlying sense of "is that all?" Richard Florida noted that meaning and purpose are "not garnered by having a 6000 square foot house, a bigger and bigger SUV and filling up on more and more consumer goods. Meaning and purpose come not from what you buy, but from what you make." When opportunities arise for us to make meaningful places, we are drawn to them.

If it is true that approximately 1% of community residents really make the community, I suspect that there are far more co-creators in New Orleans than the typical 1%. Perhaps it is due to the fact so many people left that city, and the corresponding inflow of highly motivated talent. Even people who are not typically active creators can feel the energy of the place, and that in turn inspires action. As I noted in Chapter 6, when we see others making things happen, having fun and making a difference, we want to jump in. Like a great party where many others are dancing, you are much more likely to join in the beat!

WHAT WE CAN LEARN FROM DETROIT & NEW ORLEANS

IT'S DEMOCRATIC

When I interviewed Phil Cooley from Detroit, he said something that was so simple and profound but that I had not heard in any other interview I done up until then. He said that Detroit was the most democratic city in America now. Democratic with a small "d" – not in terms of political party but in terms of its fundamental fairness and access to opportunity. Detroit, he said, was a place where anyone could play. The cost of houses or to start a business had fallen to the point where there was no reason not to get in the game. You can buy a house in Detroit for $100! Everybody has a chance to make something in Detroit. In New Orleans, Katrina washed away institutions and talent and forced the area to reset, clearing the way for massive opportunities in every area of the community. Housing prices are once again on the rise in parts of New Orleans, but the city remains affordable for the many newcomers.

"You can't change New York City. There's no land left, and it's too expensive. It's for very few people. [Detroit] is for everyone," Cooley says. "It's a democratic process. Everyone gets a say in where this city goes, the direction it heads. So, we finally can be the first potentially sustainable, socially just city in the United States."

Clearly many cities have become so expensive or so stratified that they feel very un-democratic. Cities like New York, London and Tokyo are wonderful but far from fair or easily accessible. Their exclusivity is part of their allure. But most cities are not London or New York, and those cities would do well to remind people of their democratic fairness and the opportunity to be a co-creator in their community.

PLACES NEED A PURPOSE

Larry Quick, the Australian author of *Resilient Futures* said to me "places need a purpose." When places loose that purpose, they suffer. One need only look at once great cities that have lost their purpose to appreciate the truth of this point. Take Liverpool, England. During the height of the British Empire, some 40% of world trade flowed through its docks, and as the "Second City of Empire" its wealth rivaled London's. It was even called the "New York of Europe."[95]

Today, Liverpool is a shadow of its former self, with half the population it had at its apex. Maritime trade has shifted to the ports of Asia; automobile production, which revived the region after World War II, has long since left; and the Beatles are a fond but distant memory. What then is the purpose of Liverpool? Many industrial cities in the north of England and in the Rust Belt of the United States are asking themselves the same question.

According to Eric Cedo, Detroit has a special purpose in relation to the rest of the US. "Cities, people need a Detroit to point to. The rest of the world loves a Detroit. And people say, 'Oh yeah, we love underdogs.' No. People need a Detroit because they can say, 'at least we are not Detroit.' And when you're Detroit, you don't have anyone to point to." (I live in Tampa Bay, Florida and up until 2009, there were only two major metropolitan areas in the US that did not have light rail or at least a light rail plan in the works - Tampa Bay and Detroit. In 2009 Detroit put in place a plan for light rail along the Woodward Ave. corridor and Tampa Bay became the only region with no rail plan. Even more disheartening was the failure of a ballot initiative in November of 2010 which would have added a penny to the sales tax for light rail. Detroit can point at us and smile.)

I believe the purpose of New Orleans and Detroit today is to prove to America (and to the world) that we can still build, we can still innovate and we can still do great things. New Orleans and Detroit symbolize the hopes and fears of all our communities, and if we can make them right, we know we can make our own cities great.

THERE'S AN UPSHOT...

There is a positive side of bad news. As Chris Miller noted, the steady drip of bad news about Detroit runs off those who are not highly motivated to stay and make things happen. Bad news weeds out the suckers– those fair weather fans who consume the city. And those that choose to stay are mission driven in their desire to make the city.

"You end up with some really strong, powerful people," noted Miller. "What happens if you do that over a period of 10 years? You end up with a group of people that are extremely motivated. They are determined to hold out."

Cities like Detroit, New Orleans, Cleveland, St. Louis, etc., "these cities kind of act as natural filters" according to Jeff Vines, co-owner of STL Style. "They are really good at weeding out the people who just expect everything to be spoon-fed to them, and leaving this creative underbelly of people who really understand, appreciate and really like being part of a work in progress. I think that could be an advantage."

Miller agrees: "You want the people who look at Detroit and say, 'Wow. What an opportunity.' And if you could fill your city with those people that see opportunity in the midst of disaster, that's very, very powerful."

FREEDOM

"There is far more artistic freedom [in Detroit]," says Phil Cooley. "There's less red tape. And there's still enough order. Like, the Ice House project that came into town. That was all legal. That went through the permitting process. People came in from New York, these artists, and the city opened their arms to them and said, 'OK, yes, you can close down the city. Yes, you can tap the fire hydrant to freeze this house up. Yes, you can do all this stuff.' And their permit costs, they were under $1,000 to do all this stuff for over a week."

"ARE YOU STRONG ENOUGH TO BE MY MAN?" – SHERYL CROW

Some places just feel tough and resilient. Go to the Rust Belt and you feel it in the culture there– behind the Midwestern politeness resides a strength built up from many a challenge. Mayor John Fetterman says: "When a town has gone through what Braddock has gone through, this incredible resiliency develops for those that remain."[96] You can't teach toughness, you can only earn it. As human beings we are competitive and respond to a challenge. Many places compete by telling you how good things are, how many amenities they have. Some places have to compete by challenging you. As Eric Cedo asks, "Are you tough enough to make it in Detroit?"

There is the old tale about the frog and the boiling water. Drop a frog in boiling water and it will immediately leap out. But put a frog in cool water and slowly turn the heat on and gradually bring the water to a boil and the frog will not move and ultimately perish. Most communities are facing the challenge of the rising temperature that makes them more and more uncomfortable but not so insistently pained that they are willing to take urgent, risk-taking, dramatic action.

These cities suffer in quiet desperation, dying a little everyday by the slow but inevitable accretion of global change. It is in the cities that have been shocked out of their complacency that we see the potential power that resides in every community. "Lots of people feel like things are on fire here... It is a very rare opportunity to rebuild a city from scratch. It draws ... visionaries and builders," said Kirsha Kaechele of New Orleans. The challenge facing most of our communities is to muster the will to change without facing a disaster.

Politely we call this a "can do" attitude but in reality it may be closer to a "Why the hell not?" attitude. Crisis, urgency, risk and lack of other options can make for a potent mix if one is willing to embrace it. Cities like Detroit and New Orleans have had no choice in the matter while others dance around the uncomfortable truth and seek a safer option. Again like the frog in the slowly boiling water, can your community muster the will, the strength to try something different or will half measures and safe, predictable and established techniques rule the day?

AND THE MOST IMPORTANT LESSON... ONE PERSON CAN MAKE A DIFFERENCE

Every community has people, often lots of people, who are passionate supporters of it. Yet most communities have not figured out how to tap into them as a development resource. Journalist John Gallagher, author of *Reimagining Detroit: Opportunities for Redefining an American City* notes, "One of the important lessons about Reimagining Detroit is that individual effort does make a difference, even in the face of overwhelming, impersonal forces."[97] Most of us think we have little power or influence over the cities we live in. They seem too big, too complex and too indifferent to our efforts. But some cities, perhaps out of necessity more than a grand plan, have had to open themselves up to the creative capacities of their people.

Detroit and New Orleans have become laboratories for new ideas and playgrounds for new actors. When we see the impact that individuals and small groups of committed citizens are having in these cities, it is inspiring. For most of us, the idea that we could be city builders and co-creators is a forgotten possibility. When I talk to Phil Cooley, Claire Nelson or Robert Fogarty, I am reminded that I can make a difference and that I am either part of the solution or part of the problem. Hopefully this book and the examples it highlights will encourage citizen actors to take up a cause and stimulate communities to find ways to work with such people to turn them into a powerful resource of change.

Chapter Nine
Spreading the Love -
Engaging the Co-Creators

If we accept that co-creators play a valuable role in the making of communities, then the role they play is too important to leave up to chance or serendipity. But making an effort to engage these co-creators and get them to "spread the love" is different from tackling other community issues. First and foremost, these co-creators can't be ordered to be creative. They aren't motivated by typical inducements (though money can help facilitate their dreams and desires). Co-creators need to wooed into action. You might say they need to be seduced!

The first step in any plan to support the creativity of current and would-be co-creators should be to identify them. Some co-creators will be obvious presences in a community, but many will exist "underground," like French resistance fighters. Start with the recognized co-creators, who have already established themselves over time. They will circulate in different sectors of your community, and they will often also be known as connectors who span those sectors. Go to Detroit, and people will tell you to meet Phil Cooley or Claire Nelson. Come to St.

Petersburg, and Bob Devin Jones will be on your list of must-make connections. From these hubs—the major, established co-creators—request introductions to "connect the dots." Once you find one of these "hub" co-creators, they will lead you to others because co-creators often know others of their tribe.

Once you have identified a number of co-creators, look for ways to spotlight their efforts, particularly those who may not have gotten the recognition that others have received. They're not likely to admit it, but recognition fuels co-creators even though it is hardly ever their sole motivation. Because co-creators are typically motivated by an irrepressible, intrinsic drive, a little recognition goes a long way! When I asked Phil Cooley about the tremendous amount of press coverage he has received, he shrugged it off, suggesting that he was getting too much credit and that others should be highlighted. Cooley recognized that simple praise for a job well done, and perhaps even a "thank you" of some kind, goes a long way in this ongoing battle for the hearts and minds of the community. If you tell someone that they did something that you enjoyed, that you learned something from, that got you inspired or even that you just thought they did something cool, you can make that person's day and give them the motivation to do it again.

There is also a healthy element of peer competition among co-creators. When I produce a Creative Cities Summit, one of the best things I can hear, coming from an attendee or a speaker, is a simple thank you or that they connected with someone or some organization at the Summit who is now a collaborator of theirs. News like that is pure music to my ears because it makes me feel like I am making a difference. But when another co-creator tells me that I've made a difference for them, that is the ultimate compliment. Co-creators strive for peer recognition because other co-creators understand the efforts we've made in a way that most others do not. Many artists say that they make work for other artists, for the recognition of a small group of peers— peers who don't necessarily share the same style, medium or genre, but a common trait of creative expression.

In the game of community development, creative contributors are answering the call because of motivations other than the traditional factors of money and power. That's good news, considering that both of those resources are diminishing at an alarming rate in many communities. But every community has the ability to showcase local efforts, to give praise and to say "thank you." The rest of the community benefits from learning about the people who are its co-creators and their projects— and perhaps, in seeing what their friends and neighbors have accomplished, a few more people will be inspired to join their ranks.

NETWORK THEM

Once you have identified your community's co-creators and begun to recognize their efforts, help them get connected to each other – this includes the ones who don't already know each other and those that already have some connection. When I travel to cities as a consultant, I often get to meet many of the most innovative and creative people, the people doing the most interesting stuff, in a community. In bringing them together, I am always surprised by how often they don't know each other and their respective work. Though being a connector is a common characteristic of a co-creator, hardly anybody knows everybody in practice. Don't assume that all of your community's co-creators already know each other— instead, figure out ways that they can meet. Once new connections have been made, or old ones renewed, co-creators may find ways to collaborate and to co-create amazing opportunities for the community.

"STIMULATE" THEM

Why "stimulate" and not "motivate"? For co-creators, identity is often tied to making things and, therefore, not to the traditional motivational carrots and sticks. That's not to say that money, for example, has no place whatsoever in the equation. Throwing money at these co-creators will have an effect, but for the most part you can't pay these people to do something that they don't already want to do. You could not have paid Phil Cooley to move to Detroit and start rehabbing his neighborhood; you could not have paid Phil and Marnie Holoubek to create the Lexington Young Professional Association when they moved to Kentucky. You could not pay Cherylyn Tompkins to become Miss FabuNOLA. They do these things because of who they are.

The intrinsic nature of their motivation means that co-creators are typically immune to the traditional levers that cities wield like grants, tax incentives, positions or even the key to the city. So what does move them? Stimulation – energy, excitement, fun and other activity all move co-creators to action. When they see other people making things happen, when they see other cool stuff being done, when they see opportunities to add to the mix, these people want to jump in. They want to join the party and dance too. This is why activity is so important. Activity stimulates more activity.

The opposite is true as well. When energy and life has left a community, extraordinary efforts may be required to get it back. Why is it so hard to revitalize moribund downtowns and neighborhoods? Because you are trying to create a pulse in an area that has metaphorically flat-lined. As any viewer of TV medical dramas knows, once a patient flat-lines, resuscitation takes vigorous chest pounding and even electrical shocks to accomplish, if it is possible at all. Those unsubtle efforts represent a last ditch effort to ignite something, anything. Sustaining community growth requires a more nuanced approach, more like civic acupuncture than an electric shock. But hey, if you are really trying to kick start a dead community, a fist or a car battery may be the best tool you've got.

Claire Nelson, owner of the Bureau of Urban Living in Detroit, has her own simple formula for stimulating people and the city. Step one, according to Nelson, is to get people to go out to a downtown restaurant. Next, get them to volunteer for something like a community garden project. You know people are engaged, she explains, when they start using first-person pronouns about the city, saying "we need to do something" rather than "they need to do something" about a problem.

Nelson and others like her are "urban sherpas" or city ambassadors for many who want to engage with Detroit. "My shop, the name of it, the Bureau of Urban Living, is not a great name for a shop," Nelson says, "but it works for me because with the sign out front a lot people get confused about what we are. Often people wander in because they think we are a real estate office which is just fine by me, because I get to tell them why it's great to live in the city, what housing options are available, and I connect them with my realtor friends, and we start conversations about living in Detroit... It gets to be an orientation space and community information hub... People come by just to find out what's going on in the city, and that is my favorite part of the job."

Nelson and others like her have become beacons of activity and inspiration. They have been "stimulated" into the game and now are running with it in ways that their cities never could have imagined private citizens acting.

HOW DO YOU FIND MORE PHIL COOLEYS & HALLIE BRAMS?

"What Detroit needs is 1,000 more Phil Cooleys," said Karla Henderson, director of the city's Buildings & Safety Engineering Department. "And if we get them, I tell you, we're going to be fine."[98] Henderson made that remark in the context of an interview about the growing number of do-it-yourself entrepreneurs emerging in Detroit. In New Orleans, Tim Williamson of Idea Village, put a similar idea into personal terms. "What was missing in New Orleans was more people like us," he says.[99] So how does a community find more socially-minded, high-energy entrepreneurs like Cooley and Williamson— or Hallie Bram in Cleveland or Bob Devin Jones in St. Petersburg? I know that Cooley and Bram don't like being singled out in this way—they see their efforts as part of a broader community, but they also accept such appreciation gracefully in recognition that what they do, as individuals, makes a difference.

Many potential champions and co-creators don't think the community wants or needs their help. And many cities make the mistake of not asking for help! Kim Huston from Bardstown, KY, notes that when she and the city actually asked for help and input from people on how to improve their city, they got an amazing response. "People don't think they have the knowledge or experience to share their thinking with local government," she says. "So we asked, and they shocked us with their excitement. And they loved that we cared enough to ask." Give citizens some confidence that their input is valued in the process of city making and they can become fantastic resources.

Newcomers are just waiting to be tapped as potential co-creators for any city. Claire Nelson moved to Detroit from New York City just nine years ago. She noted that Detroit "needs people [who are] not from here... We have a unique perspective. Native Detroiters see the city different from outsiders. Outsiders see the city with a bit of naïveté and a sense of urgency."

We also need to accept that co-creators may come from unlikely places and may not look or act like typical city-makers. Because they are a critical resource, judging these books by their covers may mean missing a major opportunity for the city. Some co-creators come with wild tattoos, giant earrings, piercings, or a less-than-corporate sense of fashion. Some may even come with a criminal past.

REFORMERS AND PAST TROUBLE MAKERS

Few places in the Western world are more complex and baffling to outsiders than Northern Ireland. The "Troubles" dating back to the late 1960s mark only the most recent interval in a long history of violence and conflict between various communities, including Protestants and Catholics, in that country. What many struggle with is the idea of white Catholics fighting with white Protestants, and in my years of working there, I continue to learn more and try to understand the historic, cultural, economic, social, religious and class conflict that is Northern Ireland.

The crucible of conflict, tragic as it is, has created some powerful and passionate champions, who often risk life and limb to better their community. Many of these men and women were once on the wrong side of the official law, and many admit to being engaged in the heart of the sectarian conflict at some point or another in their lives. One man, Alan Oliver, a self- described "former combatant" (meaning he was involved with a paramilitary organization) told me that he was "once part of the problem" and now wants "to be part of the solution." Today he runs a church- based program for families in the North Armagh region of Northern Ireland.

Another friend of mine, Tyrone Parker of Washington, DC, is a former felon who served 12 years for armed robbery. Prior to that, he was a very angry young man. During an interview, he recalled setting fire to buildings in the city and getting shot by a police officer during the 1968 riots that followed the assassination of Martin Luther King, Jr. Today Parker and his former gang rival, Arthur "Rico" Rush, run one of the most effective gang mediation and gang mitigation programs in the U.S., The Alliance of Concerned Men. They work in the same challenging neighborhoods that they once fought over and even razed by fire.

Why do former "troublemakers" sometimes become powerful co-creators? I suspect that they feel some guilt, some sense of debt, to the communities where they once wreaked havoc. My sense of the men mentioned above is that they are deeply motivated by a sense of personal honor. They are acutely aware of their past and are now making extraordinary, even heroic, efforts to make things better. Oliver candidly speaks of his violent history; Parker and Rush admit to their personal failures and losses. From these deep wounds emerges an uncommon resolve to do good and to prevent others from falling onto a wayward path. Some communities would choose not to engage with former criminals and men of violence— and that choice is certainly defensible. But I would suggest that communities look at these reformed citizens on a case-by-case basis and recognize that in this unlikely pool there may be some true gems who are capable of doing great things for their city.

WHEN THE CO-CREATOR RUNS OUT OF GAS

What happens when a co-creator runs out of gas? Gets married? Has kids? Is somehow diverted from her mission? Of course these changes must be seen as a natural part of the co-creator life cycle. Recall Teresa Greenlees, formerly of Tampa and now of New York City. "I remember being 28 years old six years ago and how exciting it was to create something—and how I had this fire in me to do something for the people that believed in the same things that I believed in," she says. "I don't know if I have that fire anymore." Since moving to New York, Teresa notes, "all of my creative energy is going into the work that I do. I deplete my resources in the office and then I don't have as much ambition outside of it." Phil Cooley from Detroit, Robert Fogarty from New Orleans and Hallie Bram of Cleveland all noted that their experiences in major cities like New York and Boston were similar in that they expended major amounts of energy just to keep up with their work in those cities.

For co-creators like Greenlees I believe they may be hibernating rather than exiting the stage. There are periods in everyone's life when the requirements of a job, education or family take precedence over other activities. But that co-creative impulse and the experience of making things happen doesn't go away. I prefer to think that Greenlees and others like her are replenishing their creative ammunition and that when the time and opportunity arises again, they will once again emerge as civic players. Once you get it in your system, the urge to co-create is like a benign form of malaria. Periodically it flares up!

Thankfully, co-creators are a self-renewing resource. In doing what they do, they inspire and encourage others to become active in the co-creative process. By the time they run out of gas (or go into hibernation), they have probably started enough creative fires burning in other people so that the process will continue. Creativity is a natural resource but unlike oil or coal, the more of it you use, the more you generate.

THE ONE-TENTH-OF-ONE-PERCENT SOLUTION

I've already described how small percentages of people are actually responsible for making communities, such as the 1% that made Wikipedia. We have seen how a small group of committed citizens (thank you, Margaret Mead) who are in love with their city can make remarkable things happen. Every city has some of these people, and if every city sought to identify, connect and encourage them, whole new areas of creative activities and development could flourish at little or no official cost – leaving money to fill those pesky potholes! What if we were able to increase that core group of co-creators by just 10%?

In a city of a million people, 1% equals 10,000 people. One tenth of that one percent is 1000 people. Now, that still sounds like a lot of people, so it is important to look at the actual sizes of our cities to better understand the numbers at stake. Of more than 35,000 cities in the US, only nine actually have a population of more than a million people. In fact only 279 cities of those 35,000 have a population of 100,000 or more.[100] So a better number to wrap our heads around might be a population of 100,000. Far more common than a million-person population, it is also far more manageable. With 100,000 people, when we take one tenth of one percent, we get 100 people. That is a number that we can easily wrap our heads around. (The average Facebook user has 130 friends![101])

When we talk about attracting and retaining talent, we tend to think in large numbers, e.g., thousands. But following the .1% rule, I propose that a medium sized city could significantly increase its energy, enthusiasm and creativity by adding only a hundred, or a few hundred, passionate co-creators, rather than vast numbers of city consumers and worker bees. For cities that have been trying to attract and retain large numbers of talented people, this approach offers a more attainable and targeted approach to that issue.

City	Population	1%	Tenth of 1%
St. Petersburg, FL	248,098	2,480	248
New York, NY	8,363,710	83,630	8,363
London	7,556,900	75,569	7,557
Lexington, KY	296,545	2,965	296
McPherson, KS	13,770	137	13
Detroit, MI	912,062	9,120	912
Cleveland, OH	433,748	4,337	433
New Orleans, LA	336,644*	3,364	336

    * 2008 estimate Post-Katrina

Following the .1% formula, it would take 912 Phil Cooleys to make the game-changing difference Detroit needs. (When Karla Henderson said Detroit needed a thousand Phil Cooleys, she was being more accurate than she realized!). St. Petersburg needs 248 more Bob Devin Joneses, and Cleveland needs 433 more Hallie Brams. Think of adding co-creators to a community in terms of preparing a great dish. When you are cooking, you don't need, or want, a lot of the most powerful spices to make a great dish. In cooking and in community building, a little bit of the right ingredient can be the magic element that brings all of the other flavors together.

Most of the time, small communities feel that their numbers work against them, especially when they play the amenities game and compare themselves to larger metro areas. Feeling, as the "little guy," that you can't compete with bigger cities is inevitable. Size has huge advantages, and there is a significant amount of momentum that corresponds with size. London, NYC, Chicago are leviathans that can (and do) gain and loose thousands of residents on a daily basis without feeling the drain (or the gain).

When communities engage in talent attraction and retention strategies that target knowledge workers, the highly skilled or the "creative class," they generally want to capture as many of them as possible. (And according to Richard Florida, there are more than 40 million of those people, or 30% of the total US workforce – a pretty big pool!) This view—more is better—results from the fact that most of our economic development metrics are quantitative; we measure gross numbers of jobs created, the number of people moving into the region, the numbers of businesses created and the numbers of degrees graduated. Attraction strategies typically focus on promoting cities as "amenity rich" by virtue of major cultural and civic resources. Such numbers are the net with which they hope to capture vast numbers of people, some of whom are within their targeted demographics. When smaller towns play this game, they invariably come up wanting purely because of the numbers.

"Bardstown is one of the best small cities in the US," says Kim Huston, the city's Director of Economic Development. The "Bourbon Capital of the World" boasts a strong economy bolstered by thousands of specialized manufacturing jobs in regional distilleries that produce 95% of the world's bourbon, a $1.5-billion per year industry for Kentucky. Huston is a fan of Richard Florida, but "so much of what he talks about is so far over the heads of most average-sized communities, it is hard to wrap their hands around," she says. "If you play the 'amenity rich' game, you are still compared to larger cities. How do you have the amenities of a Chicago? The answer is that you can't."

But in the area of co-creation, smaller cities can take heart.

Tom Brown is the Mayor of McPherson, Kansas, (pronounced "Mick-fur-son" not "Mick-fear-son," as I was promptly informed on my first visit, because "there is no fear in McPherson"). Prior to being elected in 2008, he worked for a decade as a consultant in China. McPherson is a town of 13,770 with a remarkably dynamic and diverse economy—and it is holding steady in population, a rare achievement among small towns in the Midwest. McPherson possesses the greatest lure of all— jobs. Their light manufacturing and oil related industries currently have hundreds of open jobs. Brown's job is to keep that growth going, and to do that he knows he needs to bring in more talent. And in order to do that, he knows he needs to build an attractive, vibrant community in addition to offering employment. But McPherson, like all cities, is struggling to figure out how to build that dynamic, attractive community with limited resources.

When Brown and I met, we discussed the idea of targeting a select group of potential co-creators and trying to encourage those people either to relocate or, in the case of potential co-creators already in the community, to take action and "get in the game." For Brown, the prospect of focusing on a key number—that one-tenth-of-one-percent—of passionate change-makers seemed far less daunting than traditional economic development metrics. "I like and appreciate Richard Florida's work, but the "creative class" view of the world is harder in places like McPherson. We just don't have the numbers and amenities that major urban areas have," Brown says. "But if I look at trying to increase my local champions, my local "co-creators" as you call them, by a dozen and have them help make McPherson a better, more interesting place to live, that seems much more attainable."

If a town like McPherson can add 13 co-creators to its mix, it would be like London adding over 7,000 creators to its community. Thirteen co-creators (recruited, empowered, unearthed or trained) can have a huge impact on the overall quality of life in the town of McPherson. This is a far more targeted and therefore achievable goal than the typical desire to "attract and retain our talent." And as the co-creators do what they do and nurture the overall quality of life, McPherson will become an even more attractive prospect for those simply looking for a job and a quality place to raise their family.

The converse of this equation holds true as well. If London loses a thousand co-creators, their absence is barely registered in the overall mix that makes up that great city. But in smaller places, the loss of even a few co-creators can have a noticeable impact. Smaller communities need to guard and cherish their co-creators and treat them the way they have traditionally treated their major employers – as if their departure could spell the difference between community life and death.

Co-creators are the makers and bringers of so much of what we love about our communities and if small towns like McPherson and Bardstown, or even medium-sized cities such as Lexington or St. Petersburg, were to adopt the strategy of increasing their co-creators and begin identifying, celebrating, networking and encouraging those people, they would soon see an amazing array of creative activities and citizen-generated resources emerge in their communities. In each and every community, these renewable resources are waiting to be discovered, cultivated and unleashed on their cities.

Conclusion

The way we think about cities centers around consumption. Consumption of culture, of resources, of infrastructure, of services. The better/easier/cheaper those consumables, the happier we are and the better we like our places. Places that cannot deliver those needs are discounted and perceived negatively.

And this is perfectly appropriate. All of us consume cities. In return we pay our taxes, we obey the laws, we behave responsibly towards each other and hopefully create some bond with our places that is beyond mere transactional convenience.

So it is not surprising that the way we rank and measure cities is based on that consumption. I picked up a magazine on a plane recently and the cover story was "100 Things We Love About New York." Of that list, most all were related to consumption in some manner (though Robert DeNiro was on the cover representing that 1%!). And again that is fine and totally appropriate. But in the new math of community building, there are numbers and elements that need to become part of the equation and the thinking we have about our places. The opportunity and ability to produce, to make things and to contribute to our places is fundamental to our human nature. Most of us will not act on these impulses but potentially all of us can. And for those that do want to make and contribute, our communities need to find ways to encourage, grow and channel this unique natural resource that is our innovative, creative and entrepreneurial capacity. As the gap between the cities we aspire to and the cities we can afford grows, cities will, out of both necessity and competitive advantage have to channel the development capacity of their citizens to fill that gap and make successful communities in the 21st century.

People in their guises as artists, entrepreneurs, activists, agitators and engaged citizens will shoulder more and more of the burden of making great cities. Official actors will continue to play their critical role but as resources become scarce and citizens use technology to create groups/movements and the tools of production become cheap and widely accessible, their official role will change. Official actors will set the standards and rules, turning the city into a platform of development that those so minded may engage with. They will become part choreographer, part shepherd, part traffic cop, part cheerleader of the creative capacity of their communities, because this creative resource will be what adds to the unique offerings of each place. The outputs of these engaged citizens will make their places authentic and distinct from every other place. And the prolific co-creators will be seen as prized community assets the way that major employers or major institutions are currently viewed. They are and will be an increasingly key part of the mix of successful communities.

To marshal these resources, we need to expand our thinking on the value of emotional connectivity and find ways to engage the human heart, which I believe will prove to be the most powerful tool ever unleashed in the development of our communities. I am not saying that "all you need is love" but I am saying that love will prove to be the difference between good enough and great, between functional and engaging, between leaving and "I think I'll stay."

When we are loved, we thrive. When cities are loved, they too thrive. When we recognize we are in a relationship with our place, we start to treat it differently and we act accordingly. When cities give back to us, even in small ways, they make themselves more lovable. When we connect with our cities on an emotional level, we are more likely to do things, sometimes extraordinary things for our cities.

The poet Giorgio Di Cicco started my thinking on this topic, so it is appropriate that he finish this book.

"When I have told you that I love you, you are closer to who you are meant to be, because you will not become your potential, who you are meant to be without being loved and feeling love"[102]

We as citizens and the cities we have built will not reach our full potential until we recognize that emotional relationship exists and that it is a central component of our lives.

Remember, every place has people who love it. Find them. Bring them together, ask them for their help. Find what is lovable about your place and make it better. Rediscover your city.

Start small. Make a simple gesture. Then another. Then another. Make it easier to make your imprint. Open your hearts and make up new things. This is our work, and frontiers are all around us.

Notes

1   Monocle, Issue 15, Vol. 2, July/August 2008

2   http://www.soulofthecommunity.org/overall-findings/

3   TED Talk - http://www.ted.com/talks/james_howard_
    kunstler_dissects_suburbia.html

4   James Baldwin, Interview by Dr. Kenneth Clark, "The
    Negro and the American Promise" American Experience,
    Public Broadcasting System, Spring 1963

5   Rusk, David. *Inside Game Outside Game.* (Brookings
    Institution, 1999) p. 90. Clarence Thomas refers to this
    phrase and writes: "Urban renewal projects have long been
    associated with the displacement of blacks; ..." Kelo v. New
    London, 545 U.S. 469 (2005) ; Alice Sparberg Alexiou, *Jane
    Jacobs Urban Visionary*, (Rutgers University Press, 2006,)
    pp 114

6   Fortune Magazine Editors, *Exploding Metropolis*, (1958) pg
    1 & 4.

7   Ibid.

8   E.L. Konigsburg, *From the Mixed-Up Files of Mrs. Basil E.
    Frankweiler* (1967)

9   TED Talk - http://www.ted.com/talks/eng/james_howard_
    kunstler_dissects_suburbia.htmll

10 Ibid

11 Ibid

12 Monocle Issue 15, Vol. 2 July/August 2008, pg. 60

13 Documentary film: Charles Landry & the Art of City Making (2009)

14 Ibid

15 Stuart Jeffries, "Why Happiness is Overrated," The Guardian, May 23, 2006 - http://www.guardian.co.uk/commentisfree/2006/jul/11/whyhappinessisoverrated

16 Magnus Gardham, "David Cameron's happiness index finds support despite impending decade of austerity," November 17, 2010 - http://www.dailyrecord.co.uk/news/editors-choice/2010/11/16/david-cameron-s-happiness-index-finds-support-despite-impending-decade-of-austerity-86908-22720393/

17 Derek Bok, *The Politics of Happiness* (Princeton University Press, 2010)

18 Robert Putnam, *Bowling Alone* (Simon & Schuster, 2000), pg 213

19 http://personaldevelopment.suite101.com/article.cfm/the_six_life_benefits_of_happiness; Martin Seligman, *Authentic Happiness* (Free Press, 2002)

20 Ed Diener and Robert Biswas-Diener, *Happiness: Unlocking the Mysteries of Psychological Wealth* (2008) pg. 52; pp 47-67

21 http://www.soulofthecommunity.org/2009/09/3-magic-ingredients/

22 Ibid

23 Ibid

24 Ibid

25 Richard Florida, *The Rise of the Creative Class* (Basic Books, 2002)

26 The Time Leader, April 7, 2010 - http://www.timesleader.
    net/articles/stories/public/201004/07/4IIU_news.html

27 http://www.soulofthecommunity.org/2009/09/smaller-u-s-
    cities-generate-more-loyalty-and-passion-gallup-com/

28 GOOD, Issue 20, Summer 2010 pg 87

29 Toby Barlow, "It Takes a Village to Open a Bistro," New
    York Times, October 24, 2009 - http://www.nytimes.
    com/2009/10/25/opinion/25barlow.html

30 Gretchen Rubin, "Cycling, Writing, Walking – and Living
    in the Right City," Psychology Today, May 28, 2010 -
    http://www.psychologytoday.com/blog/the-happiness-
    project/201005/cycling-writing-walking-and-living-in-
    the-right-city

31 http://www.google.com/analytics/

32 Data researched and compiled August 2010.

33 Michael Heaton, "Katie O'Keefe Shows Her Love of
    Cleveland With Tattoos" The Plain Dealer, July 19, 2010
    - http://www.cleveland.com/pdq/index.ssf/2010/07/katie_
    okeefe_shows_her_love_of.html

34 http://www.adiosla.com/

35 Email received from Facebook Ads Support, August 4,
    2010

36 Adam L. Penenberg, "Dr. Love," Fast Company July/Aug
    2010

37 Clay Shirky, Here Comes Everybody, (Penquin Press HC,
    2008,) pg 193

38 TED Talks - http://www.ted.com/talks/lang/eng/clay_
    shirky_how_cellphones_twitter_facebook_can_make_
    history.html

39 Ibid

40 TED Talks - http://www.ted.com/talks/clay_shirky_on_
    institutions_versus_collaboration.html

41 Jon Zemke, "Wireless Ypsilanti brings free Wi-Fi to downtown, looks to expand coverage," Metromode, February 14, 2008 - http://www.metromodemedia.com/devnews/wirelessypsi0051.aspx

42 Starbucks, June 29, 2010 - http://news.starbucks.com/article_display.cfm?article_id=411

43 Asjylyn Loder, "Louisville throws party to woo area's young professionals," St. Petersburg Times, July 22, 2008 - http://www.tampabay.com/news/business/economicdevelopment/article727067.ece

44 http://foundationcenter.org/findfunders/foundfinder/

45 http://www.bicycling.com/news/featured-stories/bicyclings-top-50

46 http://www.walkscore.com/rankings/most-walkable-cities.php

47 "Three Rhode Islanders Honored, June 29, 2010 - https://www.ri.gov/GOVERNOR/view.php?id=11710;

48 Mathew Shaer and Teresa Mendez, "Turning Cities Into Art Galleries," March 28, 2008 - http://www.csmonitor.com/The-Culture/Arts/2008/0328/p12s01-alar.html

49 American Pet Products Association, Inc. - http://www.americanpetproducts.org/press_industrytrends.asp

50 Jack Gillum, "Number of households with kids hits new low," February 26, 2009 - http://www.usatoday.com/news/nation/census/2009-02-25-families-kids-home_N.htm

51 Lisa Wood, Billie Giles-Corti and Max Bulsara, 'The pet connection: Pets as a conduit for social capital?", Social Science and Medicine, Vol. 61 (6), 2005, p. 1159-1173 & USA Today Sept 7, 2010

52 Ezra Klein, "Why Dog Owners Make the Best Citizens," Washington Post, January 5, 2010 http://voices.washingtonpost.com/ezra-klein/2010/01/why_dog_owners_make_the_best_c.html

53 Tom Van Riper and Robert Malone, "America's Most Pet Friendly Cities," October 10, 2007   http://www.forbes.com/2007/10/10/pets-colorado-economics-biz-cx_tvr_1010pets.html

54 Ibid

55 Fortune Magazine Editors, *Exploding Metropolis*, (1958) pp 164, 'Downtown is For Everyone" and Glenna Lang and Marjory Wunsch, *Genius of Common Sense*, (David R. Godine, 2009) pp 54

56 Fortune Magazine Editors, *Exploding Metropolis*, (1958) pp 147

57 Richard Florida, "Detroit: The Next American Ghost Town?" Big Think, June, 3, 2010 - http://bigthink.com/ideas/20244

58 The Gottman Relationship Institute (http://www.gottman.com/)

59 Monocle, issue 15, vol 2, July/Aug 2008 p60

60 Monocle Issue 35, Vol. 4 July/Aug 2010

61 Smart City Radio interview, Sept 2, 2009 - http://www.smartcityradio.com/show/2605/All-for-Good

62 Concept by Giorgio Di Cicco

63 Smart City Radio interview, Sept 2, 2009 - http://www.smartcityradio.com/show/2605/All-for-Good

64 Monocle issue 15, volume 2 July/August 2008

65 Monocle issue 15, volume 2 July/August 2008

66 Monocle issue 15, volume 2 July/August 2008

67 Justin Davidson , "Piazza Bloomberg," New York Magazine, Feb 12, 2010

68 Kate Taylor, "After High Lines Success Other Cities Look Up" July 14, 2010, http://www.nytimes.com/2010/07/15/arts/design/15highline.html

69 Avinash Rajagopal, "Harlem Gets its High Line," August 5, 2010, http://www.metropolismag.com/pov/20100805/giving-harlem-its-high-line

70 http://www.83degreesmedia.com/features/marry062210.aspx

71 TED Talks - http://www.ted.com/talks/nancy_etcoff_on_happiness_and_why_we_want_it.html

72 Detroit Lives - http://vimeo.com/14375565

73 Ibid

74 Toby Barlow, "It Takes a Village to Open a Bistro," New York Times, October 24, 2009 - http://www.nytimes.com/2009/10/25/opinion/25barlow.html

75 Ibid

76 Melena Ryzik, "Wringing Art Out of the Rubble of Detroit," New York Times, Aug 3, 2010 - http://www.nytimes.com/2010/08/04/arts/design/04maker.html

77 Ibid

78 504ward - http://www.504ward.com/index.php?option=com_content&view=article&id=1&Itemid=2

79 Cynthia Joyce, "New Orleans Getting Younger and Smarter," August, 29, 2008 http://www.msnbc.msn.com/id/26444928/

80 Make It Right NOLA - http://www.makeitrightnola.org/index.php/about/

81 Sloan Berrent, "Dear New Orleans, I'm Yours," The Causemopolitan, June 17, 2010 http://www.thecausemopolitan.com/dear-new-orleans/

82 "American Business: Big Easy Entrepreneurs," May 9, 2010, http://www.openforum.com/idea-hub/topics/money/video/american-business-big-easy-entrepreneurs-msnbcs-your-business

83 Abby Ellin, "Entrepreneurs Leverage New Orleans's Charm to Lure Small Business," New York Times, July 29, 2009; http://www.nytimes.com/2009/07/30/business/smallbusiness/30sbiz.html

84 Sean Callebs and Jason Morris, "After the Storm: New Orleans Economic Rebirth," August 27, 2009, http://ac360.blogs.cnn.com/2009/08/27/after-the-storm-new-orleans-economic-rebirth/

85 Abby Ellin, "Entrepreneurs Leverage New Orleans's Charm to Lure Small Business," New York Times, July 29, 2009; http://www.nytimes.com/2009/07/30/business/smallbusiness/30sbiz.html

86 Keith Bellows, "Loving the Big Easy," - http://traveler.nationalgeographic.com/2009/05/one-on-one-text/1

87 Abby Ellin, "Entrepreneurs Leverage New Orleans's Charm to Lure Small Business," New York Times, July 29, 2009; http://www.nytimes.com/2009/07/30/business/smallbusiness/30sbiz.html

88 Jason Meyers, "The New Orleans Saints," Entrepreneur Magazine, August, 2009 http://www.entrepreneur.com/magazine/entrepreneur/2009/august/202586.html

89 Richard Florida, "LeBron's Location Decision," Creative Class Exchange, July 13, 2010 - http://www.creativeclass.com/creative_class/2010/07/13/lebrons-location-decision/

90 Nathan Rothstein, "How Businesses Are Launched Big Easy Style," GOOD, April 8, 2010 http://www.good.is/post/how-businesses-are-launched-big-easy-style

91 http://www.openforum.com/idea-hub/topics/money/video/american-business-big-easy-entrepreneurs-msnbcs-your-business

92 "Either get busy living or get busy dying" - http://www.youtube.com/watch?v=hbPrVtA5v6c

93 "ToWork"-http://www.youtube.com/watch?v=635XItRDU7g

94 Melena Ryzik, "Wringing Art Out of the Rubble of Detroit," New York Times, Aug 3, 2010 - http://www.nytimes.com/2010/08/04/arts/design/04maker.html

95 The Bankers' Magazine. v.11. London (Groombridge & Sons. 1851)

96 "We Are All Workers" Episode 2 - http://www.youtube.com/watch?v=UqCqiuqDw7Q

97 Dennis Archambault, "Rethink, remake, redo: John Gallagher explores Detroit's brave new world in visionary book," Model D, October 19, 2010 http://www.modeldmedia.com/features/gallagherbook101910.aspx

98 Model D, "Rebuilding Detroit through a successful barbeque joint," May 11, 2010 http://www.modeldmedia.com/inthenews/barbque051110.aspx

99 Jason Meyers, "The New Orleans Saints," Entrepreneur Magazine, August, 2009 http://www.entrepreneur.com/magazine/entrepreneur/2009/august/202586.html

100 http://en.wikipedia.org/wiki/Table_of_United_States_Metropolitan_Statistical_Areas

101 http://www.facebook.com/press/info.php?statistics

102 TVO, Pier Giorgio Di Cicco on Being Blessed-http://www.tvo.org/TVO/WebObjects/TVO.woa?videoid?28853746001

Index

Made in the USA
San Bernardino, CA
05 October 2014